Keepers

Voices of Secular Recovery

Edited and with an Introduction by
Marty Nicolaus

LifeRing Press

LifeRing Press
1440 Broadway Suite 1000
Oakland, CA 94612-2029
Tel: 510-763-0779
Fax: 510-763-1513
publisher@lifering.com
www.lifering.com

Cover Design by Aongus Collins

10 9 8 7 6 5 4 3 2

ISBN 0-9659429-1-0

Table of Contents

Introduction

Getting sober can be a lonesome journey for the person who is underwhelmed by the Twelve-Step approach of Alcoholics Anonymous (AA). Despite significant erosion, "Step" programs still have a quasi-monopoly position in the public consciousness, and most treatment programs countenance little else. Until fairly recently, the person who did not resonate with the Twelve Step approach was more or less condemned to isolation -- rarely the best environment for long-term sobriety.

The Internet has helped to change all that. For the price of a computer and an access account, people can now quickly locate one another based on their special interests, and can link up into cyber-communities. One of these new "virtual villages" is Tom Shelley's "SOSmail" email list. This book is an anthology of selected messages posted to Tom's list during a period of nearly three years beginning in late 1996. Thanks to Tom's list and similar places on the Internet, no one with net access who wants an alternative recovery approach needs to feel isolated any longer.

As he explains in the selection that leads off the anthology, Tom was a member of a highly unusual AA meeting. Members of his group did no Steps, surrendered to no "Higher Power," and kept sober through the force of mutual support and example. Eventually Tom heard of something called "Secular Sobriety Groups," founded by James Christopher, based on the same concept. He became one of its founding members in the Tampa Bay area, in Florida.

I got sober a few years later on the other side of the continent, in Oakland, in the San Francisco Bay area, California. By that time, the "Secular Sobriety Groups" had been renamed "Secular Organizations for Sobriety" (SOS), and several meetings were already up and running locally. I attended them regularly, and still do. (Those meetings are now called LifeRing Secular Recovery (LSR).)

One evening back in about 1995, our most senior member in Oakland opined that SOS had probably ceased to exist everywhere else in the country. The SOS Newsletter had not been seen for months, and no one was answering the phone at the SOS Clearinghouse. There had been no national conference for years. None of us had personal contacts with SOS members in other parts of the country. We all carried bravely on, but the darkness moved in closer and our little candle flickered.

Eventually another issue of the SOS newsletter did arrive in my mailbox. It carried an item called "Modem Memoranda" by Tom Shelley. Tom invited people with computers and modems to send each other messages via electronic mail. I didn't really know what electronic mail was. I struggled with modem setup strings and CompuServe command codes, and after a while, I connected.

What a revelation! There were other people who felt as I did, all over the country and abroad. I could "talk" to them every day. "We" hadn't died out -- live meetings existed elsewhere. My candle brightened, the darkness receded. I became an email list regular. Participation in the list quickly evolved into an integral part of my personal sobriety program, my "Daily Do."

Inspired by the energy on Tom's list, in June 1996 I started up a web site, www.unhooked.com. One day someone on the email list wrote that a certain message was "a keeper," and how nice it would be if it got wider circulation. That was the start of the "Keepers" section on www.unhooked.com. Since then, the web site has developed into a major gateway and showcase for the email list, and the "Keepers" from the list have become a major attraction on the site. The selections in this book were first posted, with the permission of the writers, on www.unhooked.com.

As a guesstimate, I have read about 30,000 posts on Tom's list prior to preparing this volume. Why I picked this particular bunch, I can't exactly define. I'm a sucker for a good metaphor, and many of the items are here for that reason. Some of the posts grabbed me for the sheer quality of their writing. All of them, even the few that consist mainly of general reflections, have in them the flame of keenly felt personal experience. Mostly, these gems caught my eye as authentic, sparkling expressions of the three core values of this community: sobriety, secularity, and self-help.

Many of these messages are unabashed celebrations of sobriety. To a person who is still mired in drinking, abstinence sometimes seems like a drab, joyless prospect. Not so, these voices testify. Sobriety is a liberation; it is a rediscovery (or first discovery) of the senses and of the mental powers. It is an awakening of the inner potential for growth and personal development. Drinking and drugging, in retrospect, are seen as a constant hammering away at the body's pleasure system, producing eventually a paralysis of desire. It feels so good to stop doing that; it feels so amazing to experience authentic emotions and thoughts. Yes, in recovery as elsewhere, there are terrible, horrible, no-good very bad days, when the IRS calls and the battery dies and you run out of toilet paper. But at the end of the day you can still smile: you stayed sober, you are a winner. Not only can you still rock and roll sober, you can rock and roll better, and remember it afterwards.

All of these messages are secular. The writers merely express their human feelings and relate their earthly experiences. None of them asserts that the writer owns a divinely inspired recovery program, or is operating under control of a personal deity, or is having chats with supernatural powers, and the like. Maybe they believe these things, but they don't talk about them. Like an extended family at a reunion, the participants have come to agree by trial and error that personal theology is on the list of unnecessary and unwise topics. Unwise, because religious beliefs tend to cause arguments rather than to bring us together. Unnecessary, because chemical dependency is neither a sin in itself nor a punishment for our other human failings. It is one of the legion of mundane challenges to the evolution of our species. Like diabetes, psoriasis, hay fever, nail-biting, and other afflictions, addiction to alcohol and other drugs does respond to measures that rely solely on human powers.

If there is a "miracle" here, it is that the most effective engine of recovery is self-help. To secular eyes, the addict who contemplates recovery is a person in conflict. The inner capacity to get healthy is not absent; it is merely weak. The goal is for the weak and suppressed "sober self" to become stronger, and eventually to become dominant within the person. Everyone has to fight out this inner war for themselves, using the weapons and allies at hand. Some people manage to do it in isolation. Those who seek and find a compatible support group usually say that the companionship, the resources and stimulation make their individual progress more efficient and joyful. I could fill another volume with online testimonials from Tom's list to this effect.

With a few exceptions, such as "Drinking At," "Survival in the Air" and the "Holiday Survival Guide," I have not sought to string the posts together into topical threads. I did supply the titles. The items are roughly in chronological order. In this way the Internet-challenged reader can have a taste of life on the email river. You never know what's coming next, and it's up to you to gather the pieces and put them together.

Recovery groups based on sobriety, secularity and self-help are not a mere theory. They exist, they are here now. Here is a small sample of their voices. If after listening, you want to jump in, just browse to www.unhooked.com or send an email directly to the listmeister, tshelley@gte.net. To him, and to all the list members past and present, this work is gratefully dedicated.

-- Marty N.

Webmaster, www.unhooked.com

Aug. 9, 1999

Keepers

Voices of Secular Recovery

The "104" Group

By Tom Shelley

When I got sober in 1981, I was making an effort to obey the "ninety meetings in ninety days" dictum that was drilled into us in the treatment center I attended. So, being a man of economical orientation, I decided that I would find the seven meetings closest to my home. In doing this I would minimize my travel and maximize my sober contacts, as though this had anything to do with anything — I would drive fifty miles to get a drink or a bottle when the bars and package stores closed in my county.

So, as random chance would have it, one of the closest meetings to my house, on Friday nights, was the AA "104" group. As it turns out, the group took its name from a passage on pages 104 and 105 of the book "AA Comes of Age." In this book, Bill Wilson, the founder and paterfamilias of AA, said something like: "...any two or more, gathered together for the purpose of discussing sobriety may call themselves an AA group...."

The founders of this "104" group included Charles (Pappy) and Lucybelle Guckian, two of the most iconoclastic, interesting, infuriating, and caring people I have had the pleasure to meet. In short, they founded a truly secular AA group. The group operated without use of the twelve steps and without resort to the invocation of a higher power. Pappy and Lucy were ardent autodidacts (self-taught), which is a term I learned in my own self teaching. They encouraged everyone they came in contact with to learn, generally, everything that they could. Not just about the narrow focus of alcoholism, as though that weren't enough, but about every field of science, history, communication, etc. That last bit "etc." is homage to one of their favorite focuses, general semantics: a study of words, meanings, and the effects on humankind.

As you might expect, I found a home. I became a regular member of the "104" group. In the parlance of the group (and AA, in general) it became my "home group." I was steeped in the practice of making my meeting without fail, every Friday night. I was taught that sobriety was my priority (sound familiar?). This was Pappy's favorite focus. I learned a tremendous amount from Pappy, Lucy, and the dozen or so other regular members of the group. But, as often happens with many groups, the "population" of the group began to change. Pappy and Lucy left to start another meeting, closer to their home. Pappy has since died, last year at 85. The "104" group carried on for some time, though membership dwindled and we became kind of cliquish and clubby.

Relief from our doldrums came in the summer of 1987, in the person(s) of two men from Sarasota, a city about an hour south of my home in St. Petersburg. They came up to our meeting, one Friday night, because they had heard of our secular approach. They were interested and shared with us the article that Jim Christopher had written for "Free Inquiry." This word of a new "movement" happening in the home of "new movements," California, was intriguing. One of them had written to Jim for information on the nascent Secular Sobriety Groups (SSG). In turn, he passed the information on to us. I called Jim and we talked for some time. It was apparent, from the outset, that we were on the "same wavelength" and when Jim mentioned the "Sobriety Priority" I was certain that I was talking to a fellow secular sobrietist.

I need to say that starting a SSG group was not a simple decision here. For me, like for many others, I had the attitude that AA, in particular my kind of secular AA, had helped save my life. To "abandon" that and start a new sort of meeting was a bit scary. That may sound melodramatic, but it felt like we were flying solo here for quite a while. Curiously, it took many years, four or five, for the meeting to regularly get more than five or six people, even with the relatively large number of secular AA members in our area. In recent years, we have increased our membership markedly with the change of meeting days for the main secular AA group. Our meeting now boasts a number of additional members from that group as well.

All in all it has been a great and wonderful experience. I want to thank everyone, here on the SOS E-Mail List, for helping to keep this alive and make it grow.

I apologize for the length of this piece. Please don't anyone ask me what time it is.

10/10/96

My SOS One-Two-Three

By Marty N.

Four years ago yesterday I had my last drink. Today, on the fourth anniversary of my sobriety, my wife and two boys and I went out after soccer practice to a local Mexican restaurant and celebrated with lemonades and root beers. Afterwards I cleaned my toolbox in the garage, and then read my youngest a portion of The White Seal by Kipling for bedtime. Now my wife is correcting her Oakland third graders' reading homework, and I'm in bed next to her trying to put the how and why of my sobriety down on my laptop.

I had a lot of help and support getting here. My boys, especially the oldest, helped to get me across the threshold of Kaiser to seek help, and have been enthusiastic supporters of my sobriety all along. My wife and I went through some very rocky times along around year 2 and part of 3, but we have come out on the other side. She considers my sobriety the biggest gift she could have had, and from her I hear a series of stories about other marriages where the man drinks and maybe also abuses the wife and kids, and all the problems they have, that we don't, thanks to my sobriety. She makes me feel good.

My biggest debt, though, is to SOS. SOS showed me the basic human respect of not presuming to know all my problems in advance and of not having a ready-made formula to fix me up. Instead of trying to sell me a panacea or recruit me into a cult, SOS laid back and let me find my own feet. With a cunning that it took me years to discover and to appreciate, SOS understood that the only program for recovery that works for you is the one you fashion for yourself because you really want it. SOS for me has not been a ready-made off-the-shelf treatment program, but rather a safe and rich environment in which I could devise a treatment for my own self. Safe, because I have learned in these meetings that no matter what I say and reveal about my inner hurts, no harm will come to me. Rich, because by listening to the other participants and reading the literature, I have available to me a wealth of insights, tools and methods for overcoming my enemy within, and for leading a sober life.

It probably took me six months of going to two SOS meetings a week, and going to four or five Kaiser meetings on top of it, before the coin dropped in my head and I "got" the fact that I was an alcoholic. Prior to that time I had believed that to be an alcoholic was to be a bad person, or a moral weakling; and this impression was reinforced by my peripheral acquaintance with the literature of AA, with its emphasis on "character defects" and its rituals of blame and shame. As long as this was my concept, I knew I was not an alcoholic, because I knew that I was not a bad person and that I was not a moral weakling, or lacking in will or resolution of character. What I finally got clear is that I was organically damaged, either by heredity or by acquisition, and that my body did not process alcohol the same way as normal people did. My body lacks the "stop" switch that naturally and without effort of will quenches normal people's desire to drink as their blood alcohol levels rise. That limiting circuit is absent or broken in my system. As a consequence, I can never safely drink again. Although I am liable to clean up the messes I made while drunk, like anyone else, I am as blameless for my inability to control my intake as an incontinent is for his inability to control his output. We just don't have the mechanism.

Around the time I came to this realization, I had a client who suffered from Duchenne's syndrome; he was wheelchair bound, unable to control his functions, and most of his bones stuck under his skin at odd angles. Yet, though he could barely write and could not keep his head up for long, and had at age 29 outlasted the average life expectancy of persons with his condition by more than a decade, he had a clarity of mind and a ferocity of spirit that all who knew him admired. In the brief contact we had before he succumbed, following a traffic collision, I came to see that the disability of the sober alcoholic is a feather-light cross to bear, by comparison. All that we cannot do in our lives is drink alcohol or use drugs. How many would gladly trade their disability for ours!

Once I 'got it', once I understood and accepted that I was an alcoholic, the rest came easier. Over the course of the following months, I pieced together for myself a self-treatment program that perfectly suits my individual history and situation. I would like to share it, in a few words, with others on this list, by way of passing along some of the helpful points that others passed down to me.

Number one, I try to do something every day to remind myself that I am an alcoholic and cannot drink or use, no matter what. Jim C. makes a big point of this in all his writings, and his Triumph workshop constitutes the industrial-strength version of such an everyday denial-buster. (We also have the Journal of Sobriety for those who like to work with pens and pencils.) At first it was drinking decaf in the morning, instead of caf, that reminded me. Then I started taking B-complex vitamins to restore my depleted body chemistry, and swallowing those horse-sized pills every morning definitely jogged my brain. Moreover, the vitamins turned my urine neon-yellow, so that the reminder repeated itself throughout the day. Then I mentally associated tooth brushing with affirming my alcoholism, and that worked for a time. Lately I've been using my participation in this email list as my Daily Do. A few months ago my wife took a weight reduction class, and the instructor there, in a very similar vein, gave them a long list of healthy eating practices and told them they had to do Something Of Something ("SOS") every day. So, having an everyday ritual of affirmation, a daily denial of denial, is a very "SOS" thing to do.

Number two, I try to participate regularly and actively in SOS meetings. Fortunately our meetings are small enough where you cannot sit behind a pole and daydream. This was hard for me at first, as I was not accustomed to revealing feelings or speaking about myself in meetings, and I resisted it. Even after four years it sometimes takes me nearly the whole meeting before I can open up inside and share. One of my Kaiser counselors pointed out once that our feelings are one of the few things in life that we can change by merely talking about them, and this is true for me. If I am feeling lonely or depressed, or stressed, or ashamed, or guilty, I can unload the poison from those feelings by sharing them with the group. This helps to relieve emotional stresses that might drive me to drinking. Sometimes just saying "Hi, I'm Marty, I'm an alcoholic" in front of my friends at the SOS meeting is all that I need to do. Often it's the things that come out of my mouth unsuspected that help me change, more than the things that come into my ears. Participation in meetings also helps me regain basic social and psychological skills, stunted during years where the bottle was my best and only friend. Active participation strengthens my ability to empathize with others, and my ability to ride out and accept my own feelings without panicking and reaching for an anesthetic. In these and other ways that I am only beginning to understand, participation in SOS meetings has helped me not only to stay sober, but also to recover from the damage I did myself during my three decades of active alcoholism.

Three, I've discovered for myself that the famous Sobriety Priority is a hell of a useful way to analyze what I do in life. As Jim C. has written so many times, we prioritize sobriety as a separate issue so that we do not drink or use, no matter what. When I drank, almost everything I did had drinking connected to it as a separate issue. Now that I am sober, almost everything is related somehow to sobriety. I can view the flowchart of my life as a series of decisions, some of whose branches tend to lead toward sobriety and others toward relapse.

The Sobriety Priority is a bright line through the blooming, buzzing confusion of life. There are a few days when I find my brain doing this kind of analysis, applying the Sobriety Priority, hundreds of times. You might be amazed at the kind of problems the Sobriety Priority algorithm can analyze and solve!

Taken together, my One, Two and Three form a closely knit matrix of support for my sober life. Both my mind and my feelings are engaged. My personal program involves both my inner and my outer relations. There's something sober I do twice weekly, something sober I do daily, and something sober I can do anytime or all the time. So, as near as I can figure it out, that's how I've managed, after thirty plus years of drinking, to get sober and stay sober for four.

And now I promise to shut up and never again to post a 'share' this long, except maybe on my next anniversary, if I make it that far. Thank you all for your support along the way.

(Posted 10/2/96)

A Loner in Sweden

By Jan A.

Many years ago I became intellectually clear over that I was an alcoholic. I belonged to the 10% of the Western population that had no mechanism to stop drinking once started. Conclusion: Don't ever drink alcohol! - Easy to say. However, I had studied articles and books about the Minnesota model and I guessed that the most effective part of the treatment was that alcoholics came together. They talked about their experiences of drinking and their hopes to get rid of this heavy burden.

At the same time research has showed that a main factor causing alcoholism was the personal genetic constitution. Alcoholism was not bad moral and insufficient self control. Alcoholism could be regarded as a "bad construction" like diabetes or as a sickness. We alcoholics got more self respect by hearing this but the problem was still there.

I had only vaguely heard about AA at that time, so I didn't join a group. Maybe there was none to find in my town. Instead I started talking with alcoholic friends about trying to stop drinking. Most of us really wanted to achieve sobriety. During these talks and discussions I was sober all the time. Weeks added to months and I was still sober. Sometimes I had to help my friends to the detox clinic. Of course I sometimes was tempted to drink during that time but I could manage it by reading the literature of the Minnesota model.

After about three years in this sort of living I met a neighbour at my summer house. We came to talk about "life" and he told me that he was a sober alcoholic in AA. I told him that I had the same problem but that I was on my way out from active alcoholism. He asked me to go with him to an AA meeting this evening. I did and I was rather impressed of the friendly and calm atmosphere of this meeting.

Then I joined AA for many years - a group had started in my home town. When I told my story about my way to sobriety I was always told that I wasn't really sober - I had only fought with "white knuckles" during these years outside AA. I still get angry hearing such nonsense - I had rather had a harmonic time with my alcoholic friends and with myself. A demanding time and a lucky.

Being a non-believer wasn't always easy in AA. So much talking about God and the HP and at the same time AA had no connection to any sect (The Preamble). Lots of contradictions. Since I was a teenager I have had a secular view and this caused me intellectual problems all the time. At same time: AA was the only game in town. And I had got friends there who I really could rely on. I needed the friendly talking and these weekly sessions of good humor and discussions of important topics. I STILL NEED IT! It is rather curious; some members of AA are atheists, other agnostics, some true believers, others who want to believe but can't and some who think they are God themselves. All these people seem to get along in some way or another within AA.

A few years ago I got a new problem with AA. I was elected a member of the Literature Committee of central AA in Sweden and now one had decided to make a new translation into Swedish of the Big Book (the latest American edition). I wasn't directly put to work with the translation but I had to give my opinion about the translation and to help find suitable Swedish wordings when the translators were in doubt. It became more and more trying to be involved in this work. How could I have an opinion about religious matters that I regarded as nonsense? I decided to resign recently and I am happy for that.

Since I connected to Internet about a year ago I have checked homepages concerning humanism, skepticism and recovery from "-isms". I found SOS on the net this autumn and here I am. I STRONGLY BELIEVE THAT MY WAY TO SOBRIETY WAS THE WAY SOS TELLS US IN PRIORITY ONE. The only difference is that I had no name on my own way. My sobriety has to date lasted more than 16 years, so I am convinced that Priority One is the right way to follow. AA helped me in many ways during the years - you need friends along the road. I have read the books by James Christopher and I am a strong supporter of SOS.

I wish I could start SOS groups in my home country. Maybe I can, but it will take a lot of time. Although many Swedes are able to read and talk English, we can't have our meetings in English. We need to translate a lot of the available original literature (with permissions re copyright, of course) into Swedish. I cannot do it myself, I am 68 and have even other things to do. I guess that I must first send out the message that SOS exists and get some fellows joining me and SOS. When we are a gang here that can keep contact with one another and when the circumstances are favourable to get something successfully done, then it is the right time to start.

In the nearest future I have to be a "loner" in Sweden but it will be OK now that I have joined this group in the listserve.

I thank you all and I wish you all the best and I'm looking forward to taking part in this forum.

Tag inte den foersta! (Don't pick up the first one!)

Jan Armann, Sweden

Aug. 1996

Kerrville, Texas

By Paula B.

> *Nick J. wrote: To get to where I live, go up to I-10, take a left, go past Houston (where I suspect Charles is), then about an hour past San Antonio (Kerrville). I still think AA chapters that don't hold the Big Book and the 12 steps as sacrosanct must be in a rather small minority. -- NickJ*

Nick, Sorry, dear - Come to Tampa, get Paula & Karen together & we'll figure out how to get you to Kerrville. First you find a beatup Ford pickup, driven by our grandfather (Popie), make sure it has a bed full of happy & singing children. If you can hear the childish voices clearly, they'll (we'll) be singing the old Methodist hymn - "Climb, Climb up Tivy Mountain". Follow us, as we drive (somehow, in Kerrville), up a winding road with gears grinding, and Popie laughing & wiggling his ears, and Texas dust covering us all. We get to the top (top is a relative term) and we laugh and dance & sing - Popie says, "let's go get lemonade'...we cheer & get back in the truck & go back down the mountain. When we got back down, Gagie would greet us, looking stern because Popie wasn't supposed to take the kids off like that. We'd go next door, or hide in the brush, or go in for a nap & when it blew over, Gagie would give us hot cornbread with butter, or sweetpotato pie. I started my first period in Kerrville. My sister, from whom I had previously withheld nothing, asked me what it felt like. I couldn't tell her how confusing and annoying & uncomfortable the whole business was. I think, before that, she & I were partners in my family. When I became a woman, we were no longer. Gagie pulled me into her lap in her rocker in that house in Kerrville. Gagie wore a girdle for shopping, for church, for any appearance outside her house. She wanted to teach me about being a woman. I remember she smelled of powder and soap. She was so soft - we were home,after all. Gagie - Florence Lively Miles - told me about being 15 & starting to menstruate in a world where women used rags & then washed them in sinks & hung them on a line in private, so as not to annoy their menfolk. Gagie told me to watch myself at all times, because now that I was a woman, I had to be careful. She told me to pray & to be good. All I really knew was that she loved me, that my tummy hurt, and I had breasts that suddenly hurt & I didn't like most of this attention. I was eleven years old, I had attempted suicide for the first time a few short months ago because I was being moved to Taipei, and Kerrville was my last image of home.

(10/25/96)

No More Time Outs

By Dudley A.

In my youth (when I was 54 — 8 years ago) I discovered that I had a problem with excessive alcohol consumption, a condition which seemed to worsen with age because when the kids left home and the dog died I felt there were no longer any restrictions on how much booze I could consume.

Like anyone else new to the game, I felt it would be appropriate to seek help from those who should know how to deal with such conditions, to wit: AA and the rehab industry.

After very brief dealings with both, I concluded that I didn't want to get involved with a Jim Jones mindset merely to stop drinking. Accordingly I decided to stop without any assistance from the "experts."

I did help get an SOS group going here in Atlanta and for that matter still attend - not because I am "recovering" from anything, but simply because I rather enjoy an intelligent conversation from time to time and I feel it important for newcomers to observe first hand that there is indeed life after booze.

This morning I worked out with my weights and stair stepper for about 1/2 hour, rode my bicycle to the tennis courts (only about 3/4 mile) and then played tennis until noon. This afternoon I did some volunteer work for a couple of hours, played CPA for a while and then got involved with this computer gadget. Tonight it was my turn to cook so I spent some time preparing a nourishing meal for my wife and me. Last week I had a complete physical and it was determined that I was disgustingly healthy except that I still have a problem with shortness of breath as a result of smoking 3 packs of Marlboros for as long as I can remember. (I gave up the cigarettes 6 years ago.)

Eight years ago the only exercise I ever got was bending my elbow, and eating was something that was done only out of necessity; neither the taste of the food nor the nourishment provided seemed to have any relevance. What was important was that I could start drinking after work — and the hell with the rest of the world. I was always too embarrassed to have my blood pressure taken by a doctor so would volunteer to give a pint of blood. Sometimes they took it and sometimes they didn't, but the important thing was that I didn't have to answer any questions.

Any of this sound familiar?

I, of course, was not an alcoholic but suffered from a "Designer Impairment" because I never hit rock bottom nor got a bunch of DUIs and that sort of thing. (I did drive into a tree on one occasion and into a house on another, but that was because I was dealing with "stress"!) In some circles I am suffering from Denial, but between you and me I've enjoyed every minute of it — for a total of eight years.

When I first had to confront my reality I read everything I could about "alcoholism" but avoided all of the traditional crap which smacked of a religious resolution. If Columbus and I were the only ones who refused to join the Flat Earth Society, then so be it. It was a very enlightening exercise, but in the end the issue I had to resolve was one of control; either the booze was going to control the rest of my life or I was. I decided on the latter, and the rest wasn't all that big a deal. (I've always maintained that sobriety gets easier with age because you're in the fourth quarter and you're out of time outs).

(10/28/96)

The Worst Week of My Life

By Gary S.

In 1987, I was a 29 year-old optical engineer at a large aerospace company in So. California. Although I was making good money at that time, we never managed to accumulate anything. My wife Kay and I lived in a two bedroom apartment which we shared with two cats (no kids yet). Every morning I would wake up with a hangover and go lean over the bathtub for about 15 minutes telling myself I had to quit drinking so much. I wasn't throwing up — just trying to wake up. There would always be some reason to start a fight with Kay before going to work. (On those rare occasions when I did not, I made note of it, and Kay always told me how "good" I was doing that morning.) The hangovers would last until about noon. Sometimes after work I would go out for a drink and wind up calling Kay to tell her I would be late (I was a very responsible drunk). Other nights I would go home and work on my computer. If I hadn't started drinking already, inevitably an alarm went off in my brain at 9:00 p. m. telling me it was time. From then on I proceeded to get drunk, although rarely to the point of blackout in the latter years. [...]

On March 3, 1987, I went to an urgent care clinic with a sprained wrist. I had a hard time getting anyone to look at my wrist since all the questions were about my drinking. Finally I was told that my liver was enlarged, and it was time to stop. My initial reaction was relief. I had known virtually since the day I started drinking that this day was coming, and when it did, I was almost glad for it to be over. Little did I know then what getting over it would actually entail.

It took two or three days for it to really hit me. I was one big raw nerve without alcohol. I believe that my brain is a very poor producer of whatever chemical it is that gives us a sense of well-being and contentment; and that it was only too glad to have alcohol take over its responsibilities in that area, so that even its limited native ability was very much diminished by alcohol. (In fact it would take almost two years for it to get back to what is normal for me, which is what I meant by "Little did I know then ...")

It was then that I sought out AA, since I had always known that AA was where you turned if you were an alcoholic and wanted to stop drinking. Now different AA groups have widely differing characters. Had I walked into the meeting I attend right now, I would probably have fit in better than I did. What I found was a group of lower bottom alcoholics and addicts. I made the following entry in my journal for, appropriately enough, Friday, March 13. (The entry was not actually made *on* that day, but recreated on March 25 from notes taken earlier — hence the past tense.)

"I decided to try controlled drinking. I was going to drink varying amounts each day according to a prescribed schedule for 12 weeks. I already knew in my mind that I was an alcoholic but I was not convinced that I was powerless over alcohol. It was hard for me to feel like an alcoholic deep down since I had not gone through the endless trying to quit and not being able to as most alcoholics have. I thought that if I made it for the 12 weeks, I would still be an alcoholic but at least I wouldn't be as bad off as those losers at AA who had to fantasize about God to keep themselves from drinking."

Most of what I know about what I was feeling at the time comes from my journal, most of which is too personal (read "embarrassing") to print, especially under the watchful eye of webmasters and newsletter editors. I cheated on the schedule only once, then made up for it the next day. My self respect required that I take only one of two actions: continue the experiment, or return to total abstinence. I ended the experiment after 1 week, which I think speaks for itself. The torture of moderate drinking was something I could not continue to bear — abstinence was far preferable.

To end the story here would make me look stronger and more noble than I deserve to look. In order to achieve "closure" with alcohol, I had to have — you guessed it — a last drunk, which I proceeded to do on Friday, March 20 — actually blacked out on that one. The next day, my OCD kicked in telling me that the "closure" had not been done well enough: there were things I had to be thinking while having that last drink. I had several drinks over the next three days trying to get it right. My most recent (dare I say "last") drink was on Monday, March 23, 1987.

Now you will no doubt think that your case is different. I was in the throes of withdrawal, while you have several years sobriety behind you. You may be right. However, any further experimentation will have to be carried out on your end. I cannot look at my history and not think that I was an alcoholic because I have a physiological propensity to alcohol addiction. My sense of responsibility, discipline, and will power were at least average, and I think above average. My brief experiment with moderate drinking was notable for its intensity, but I tortured myself for *years* with moderate smoking when I was even younger.

I would try to think of an elegant way to end this, but its late again, I have a final exam this week, and I don't want to delay getting this out any longer, so I'll just say Good Luck and Best Wishes, Gary

Dec. 96

The Meaning of Humility

By J. C.

I attend a group therapy session which meets before my Thursday SOS meeting. Last week we brought in a new member. As the session drew to a conclusion we were asked to share our favorite meeting with this new guy. Of course, I said, my favorite meeting was the SOS meeting which convened right after the therapy session and invited the newcomer to attend. This rankled one of the staunch AAers who began to proselytize about the lack of "humility" in SOS and how our program lacked "service." I asked this individual if he had any children. He answered no. I told him that I had three and that I was involved with parent organizations, sat on the board of an Education Foundation, was the past president of my homeowners association, that I coached Little League and Soccer teams and that I spend seven to ten hours a week every week working for free for the community. I also told him as an atheist I felt I had less ego than those who believe a Higher Power has time to spend time listening to their prayers and when their lives were over, was going take their spirits to heaven. I have the humility to believe, I told him, that when I die, I will disappear. All that is left is what I have passed on to the people I touched while I was here. Now, who has the inflated ego?

(3/19/97)

Letter From London

By Nick L.

My name is Nick and I am married to a recovering alcoholic named F. I just discovered your web site and I have to say the FAQ section regarding the "strengths and weaknesses" of SOS and AA just completely connected with something I'm going through at the moment.

My wife checked into Farm Place, which is the original UK 12-step treatment centre, seven weeks ago. I was delighted. She'd made the decision on her own, researched the place, arranged the health insurance to cover her stay, and had the courage to do it.

She's been a drinker all her life, and was a wild woman when I met her — one reason I was attracted to her, in fact. Then, she also used to do a lot of coke — always to excess, which was the difference between us. But as the eighties ended and we got older, she shrugged that off, we had a kid, then she tried to stop smoking and her drinking started increasing.

Then she joined AA six years ago, and began a pattern of bingeing in between periods of sobriety that would sometimes last weeks. Last year she was sober for seven months, until her father's wake in Ireland, when she was pressurized to drink 'out of respect for her father' by the locals. Three months of alternating between drinking and meetings followed.

However, after seven weeks of recovery in Farm Place, seeing her once a week and talking on the phone, I'm having serious doubts about what's going on there. It seems like the alcoholic who checked in is being replaced by an AA Moonie. Everything is based around The Big Book, to the exclusion of everything else.

To begin with, she was in tears, she wrote me saying "please write and be supportive" then, she said, she just surrendered. Now she's hard, seems to be talking Therapyspeak all the time, tells me "This all has nothing to do with you. You're not an alcoholic," has a fake smile as she listens to the kids talking when they visit, and is incredibly secret about anything going on there.

Since her drinking was (she thought) secretive and obsessional, it seems to me that one destructive problem is being replaced by another. Her life story, it seems to be, is also being "moulded" to fit the accepted wisdom that it's all been one long downward plunge into oblivion. "The last few years, I was either hung over or drunk. I didn't know who I was" she said in a meeting the other day. That's just not true. In the eighties it might have been, but recently it would only truthfully apply to about ten days in any given month.

We've run a film production company together for the last few years. We've brought up two kids. We've done film shoots all over the world. We work together for twelve hours a day. She was hung over some mornings, yeah — but for almost as many of the last seven, she's been having 'sober days' and AA meetings. The Bad years were actually 1982-88, and earlier — before our relationship actually began, when she lived with other alcoholics and did things like burn down a hotel in NYC.

"Why didn't you punch me out and lock the door when I was drinking?" she said yesterday, angry. In the evenings — only ever during the evenings, with one or two rare exceptions — she would sometimes drink two bottles of wine and quietly fall asleep, at which point I would — rather than waste my time screaming or crying — relax, get round to calling friends, work on screenplays, and generally detach myself from a problem I felt only she could actually solve. The next morning she would often be remorseful and we would discuss what could be done, which is how she eventually ended up in a treatment centre.

Now that her life is officially described as ever-mounting hell, she is furious with me for being an Enabler. I am regarded as being a "Doormat" for putting up with all this. When I say that, in my memory and a lot of my friends' memories, I recall things as being not altogether that awful - in fact, pretty damn good — for the last ten years — I am of course regarded as being In Denial. AA has a guaranteed no-lose situation here, I feel, a bit like "if she floats she's a witch and if she sinks she's innocent."

Last week, a councilor warned her it might be a good idea to end the relationship with me, since it might be a threat to her sobriety. (The councilors are delighted with her progress since she gave in, of course). "I've got step 2" she told me a few weeks ago. "What's step 2?" I asked, later. She was furious with me for intruding on her privacy. I have been given strict instructions to attend Al-Anon meetings if there is to be any chance of us saving our relationship. The two I have attended so far were, of course, full of (rather bitter) 12-steppers and slogans and higher power discussions — which I feel is even stranger when being practiced by people who aren't addicts themselves, and presumably don't have that desperate need for a Big Defined Structure to their lives. As you can see, my experience ties in exactly with the way you describe the "one size fits all" psychic curriculum, which I think is succeeding in stopping her drinking, but with some pretty drastic side-effects. I'd like to know more about SOS. Do you run a Al-Anon-type thing for families? Are your meetings open, and if so, do they exist in London?

Finally, thank you so much for letting me read something that I can really relate to on the subject of addiction and recovery.

(2/27/97)

The Happy Neurons

by Mark P.

I have been following the literature on chemical dependency for 17 years and always like to get my two cents in. Especially since this has been a topic of discussion here of late.

The nature of chemical dependency is, to me, one of nature's really fascinating stories. Why is there such a thing as addiction at all? What even makes such an odd thing possible? If you step back from it, it sure is a goofy-ass thing to have happen to anybody.

"Once upon a time".... roughly 500 million years ago, evolution came up with one of its most elegant inventions. It happened in some fish-like critter since the land wasn't populated yet. It was the evolutionary invention of the self-rewarding neuron. Imagine it. A "feel good" neuron. A way to manipulate behavior (in evolutionary terms) by having the organism reward itself!! This is, to me, one of the most interesting moments in all of evolution, because it is what makes complex behaviors possible. So here we are 500 million or so years later at the end of an intricate evolutionary shaping process.

What makes you feel good? Sex, obviously. If it weren't for these reward neurons, sometimes called reward centers, there wouldn't be 5 billion or so sapiens sapiens running around the planet. But these reward systems are much more ubiquitous and subtle. They reward us for all kinds of things from eating a good meal to doing a good job to making a friend. They regulate our social behavior in public. They make possible intricate forms of social learning. There are probably thousands of behaviors that are rewarded by our own little brains, and hundreds of reward systems to deal with them.

Remember, this has been going on for 500 million years, enough time to create some pretty evolutionarily crafty stuff. So there you are, your wife has just given birth to your first child and you see it for the first time and are overwhelmed with good feelings. Reward system in action, big time.

So how about addiction? As I mentioned there are probably hundreds of these reward centers in the brain. Certainly trillions of reward neurons coursing throughout most of the brain. When one ingests what we call addictive chemicals what happens to the brain is that most or all of the these reward centers are set off at once, in a way that was never intended by Mother Nature. The addictive chemicals bind to the receptors on these reward neurons and, if you're on this email list, you know what happens. Especially in the early stages of addiction: Euphoria. An overwhelming sense of well-being. No problems. All is well with me and the world. I look in the mirror and I am 2 inches taller and I can talk to girls at the dance...etc. The effect of all this is BAM!…new brain! The use of the addictive substances reconfigures the whole reward system of the brain. In little pieces these reward systems motivate evolutionarily productive behaviors and, as I mentioned, the success is in the pudding. Five billion or so.

But, now all of Mr. Brain's reward neurons have been set off at once and focused on the substance that did it! Holy shit, Mary. The use of the substance, because of its effects on the reward neurons, takes on all the characteristics of the strongest biological drive possible. It surpasses even the drive for self-preservation. Why? Because the brain's reward systems have been reconfigured to support the use of the substance that sets them off, in the same way that they were originally configured to reward certain behaviors, only now they have become overwhelmed, focused on supporting the use of the addictive substance. We all know what happens from that point on.

At this level of organization an addiction is a relatively simple thing to understand. At the neurochemical level it gets a little more complicated. All brains are not the same. All receptor sites are not created equal. Thus, because some molecule in a person's dopamine receptor hooks a little left instead of right, cocaine is not addictive to that person but might be to the other 80% of the population. Alcohol we know becomes addictive to those whose neurochemistry manufactures a synthetic opiate out of alcohol. We've known this for at least 26 years. Hence the reason alcoholism is hereditary. The possible neurochemistry is coded for in the DNA. It only becomes a problem when it meets alcohol.

So, is this a disease? Certain things are irrefutable. It is organic. It is biologically based. It is a functional disorder of the reward system of the brain. It alters the behavior of trillions of neurons. It causes irreversible damage. You, obviously, can't have the condition without the addictive chemical but then you can't have an allergy without the allergic substance.

I will say that, in my humble opinion, the understanding of the nature of addictions represents the finest of what science can do. Parenthetically, the most significant research wasn't done by people in the alcohol/drug field. As is often the case, old paradigms do not change from within but only change when confronted with new evidence from without.

What is not so nice is what happens in the socio/political world. It has always been difficult for Western culture, particularly American culture, to accept any behavior that is not volitional. We are, after all, captains of our destiny, are we not? There is this thing called consciousness and it is the arbiter of all behavior. That's the way it is for me, by God, and that's the way it is for you. If you're "addicted" to a substance it's your own damn fault, etc.

Most people in A.A. have no real understanding of the biology of addiction. When they talk about the disease (disease [give me a break!]) they are usually referring to some kind of characterological disorder (addictive personality or somesuch) as the disease entity. It is all very strange and, of course, interspersed with mysticism.

For some reason many individual resent the idea of being "diseased." I have never really understood why. Personally I don't give a tinker's damn that it might be a "disease." What matters to me is that there are behavioral techniques and therapies that can be used to put this thing in remission. I think I am grateful that so many people have spent so much time in trying to understand this thing and uncover its nature. It perhaps, someday, will change the attitudes of the general public toward chemical dependency. But, I'm beginning to ramble. I hope the above gives people a context in which discussion can take place about this crazy, deadly thing called addiction.

April 14, 1997

The Real Birds and Foxes

By Jerome C.

I had this idea I used to use on AAers who said I had to get spiritual to stay sober. I would say that alcohol made me very spiritual, that's why they call it spirits in a bottle. The thing I needed to do is come down to earth and get out of the fantasy, spirit filled world my mind was taking me to when inebriated. If I want to go back to the spirit world I will start taking drugs or drinking again. However, since drinking is not an option for me then.....well it's the real birds, foxes, etc in the "real" world that I will be seeing.

6/1/97

I'm Going to Be There For This Kid

By Rick G.

I thought I would take this opportunity to mention something that I noticed again yesterday. I love my new life since I quit drinking and drugging and here's one of the benefits of being straight that maybe some people in early recovery haven't noticed yet. Took me years to catch on, but most seem to see it sooner than I did.

Since all my kids grew up and moved out, I decided to move my office home. I love it (except for the traffic jam in our home) because I get to be at work and home at the same time now half of the time. But the best thing about it is my daughter brings her baby, our granddaughter, over almost every day. I can stop work and go visit.

My wife and I had two kids, but I have little idea what babies are like. You see, I missed most of that part of my kids' life. Oh, I was living at home, but I was more interested in getting loaded, and missed the REAL growing up of my kids. I didn't even realize that until our granddaughter was born about seven months ago. There I was standing in the hospital waiting room thinking "what happens next? When will they come out and give us an update? I'm so new at this and it feels great!" I realized that I had never really held a baby and played with it. I'd never fed one or changed a diaper since they didn't trust me not to drop my kids on the floor, and I'd never even looked at any other babies.

I was around for all the years my kids grew up, but I now realize I wasn't there. And for the last ten years I've been trying to make up for my mistakes by buying cars and things, creating jobs that they could do that I didn't need to have done and giving cash, instead of being there for them. I'm going to BE THERE for this kid and for my own, and for my wife from now on.

Nothing is more important than the people that I love, but I've made them play second to every whim I've ever had. By wasting time being addicted, we shortened our living lives and cheated ourselves and our families out of us.

We're going to have some tough times around here for awhile soon. I'm not looking forward to this event, but I am grateful that I'll be able to participate this time and feel the pain and loss like the rest of the human beings.

The Things I Do

By Lin L.

I used to be a religious person, believed in god and everything. Thought about becoming a rabbi (probably mostly because I like to argue). Then I learned to drink, did it too much, and found AA.

That cured me. First of all, AA is so darn Christian, that I had to question what I heard. I had to learn to filter out Moonies and Jesus freaks in college, and then AA came along and really put me to the test; after all, this was a life-or-death thing.

So, I gotta find Jesus or I'll die? Fat chance, buddy. So I objected, and got the "ketchup bottle" lines in all their myriad variations. Pray to a ketchup bottle? Not likely. After all, what interest does a ketchup bottle have in my sobriety? For that matter, what interest does a god have in my sobriety?

Doubts, doubts, doubts. Read "Came To Believe" and that pretty well trashed my "spiritual journey." Hang in long enough, listen to enough sermons, actively participate in your own recruitment, and eventually you'll agree with us.

But I'd already had a perfectly good religion, and it wasn't theirs, so why was I going along with this? For that matter, if god was so darn concerned about my drinking or not drinking, why did I develop a problem with the stuff in the first place? Maybe, I figured, the whole thing has nothing to do with god, and everything to do with the things I do. Just lil' old me.

So, while I'm still looking for evidence that a god somewhere gives a shit about anything we bizarre organisms do, I have left the search on the back burner, behind the really important stuff, like laundry.

July, 1997

It's Not Worth It

By John R.

Dear Friends, life has its ups and downs and in the last few months I noticed how depression and mood swings affect even our friends with the longest sobriety. I've started feeling a little down lately and I realized that I am lonely and miss the drinking friends I used to have. It's funny how they never call anymore. All they needed was a drinking buddy I guess. I can't fulfill that role anymore.

After 8 months of sobriety, the longest being 3 weeks prior to that in the last 20 years, I felt I had come so far and was so self-confident that I could now test my ability to drink in moderation. It started so innocently when I played golf with a local pharmacist patient at my local club and thought I'd ask her to join me for a cocktail up in the clubhouse lounge. She had a drink and I had two. She said that more than one made her sleepy. I realized then I wanted more but left with just a mild buzz. When I think back I realize that if I weren't an alcoholic I wouldn't have wanted more and would have just enjoyed the mild buzz I had. Anyway, the next day I truly believed I could control my drinking and started going to bars and buying alcohol to take home and drink. The quantity increased within a week so much that I remember waking up with a hangover and wanting to drink to relieve the symptoms. That I did. Then came the fifth a night after work to relieve the previous day's hangover and the night sweat, nausea, and diarrhea.

Finally, I was totally miserable and totally dependent and trapped on alcohol and realized that it had happened all over. Then I knew what I had to do. I had to endure the terrible withdrawal symptoms. I had been drinking a fifth of vodka a night for two weeks after a dozen other lesser drunks. The things I did during that period seem incredible now. This was from mid-May until last week. I was encouraged by the letters to Randy and quit again this week. It was terrible. I knew it would be horrible but it was worse than that. I had chest pains and almost had to call an ambulance. I quit drinking Monday at 2 pm when the bottle was empty. I knew I had to work on Tuesday and thought I could get through it. I was wrong. By midnight Monday night I was sober and feeling nauseous like hell. On the verge of throwing up, and with diarrhea every hour until my butt was bleeding and burning with tremendous pain. The nausea was so bad that at 8 am. I could still barely move out of bed to call in sick. I was totally booked up and they had to reschedule all my patients. The nausea and diarrhea finally subsided 8 hours later! I could work the next day though still hungover but am feeling better now.

The main point is ITS NOT WORTH IT TO TAKE ANY DRINKS AT ALL. The suffering is 100 times worse than the mild pleasure beforehand.

Anyway, I'm sipping chamomile tea and taking Valerian Root capsules to help me sleep at night and get over the shakes. I've been through this before and it's not fun!

July 1997

A Letter From My Father

By Robert B.

This date is a strange anniversary for me. I went down to the Outer Banks of North Carolina, and some time around noon my (ex) wife and I were exchanging vows at the Dare County court house in Manteo. Since this was back in my drinking days, the trip up to Nags Head consisted of half a bottle of Pepto Bismol to try and take care of the night before, and the ceremony was followed by a trip to the nearest bar to get where I needed to be. I had gone ahead with the trip, knowing that my dad was terminally ill at the hospital in Bethesda, Md. When we returned, I called and found out that he had died that morning. Not many folks with that distinction, I reckon. Some time much later my mom sent me some of his writings, including a letter he wrote to her brother Tommy Joe, who was having his low points at the time, and shares our (and his) "taste" for the booze. I posted this before, but thought I'd put it out again, a little reminder of how he felt about sobriety. Hope you indulge an old fart. Like father like son…

> April 26, '72
>
> Dear Tommy Joe,
>
> I remember an evening in late August of 1935 when a cocky young school teacher spent a late evening with some of his equally cocky students gulping down beer at the 24 Hr. Cafe. Late that night the teacher was still sober, sorta, and Ted Burke, Leo Klimboski and a little smart aleck were drunk. I carried the latter one home (he had some cute sisters) and deposited him quietly on the sleeping porch, hoping he would sober up in time for class the next day. He did.
>
> Tommy, I am an alcoholic. I don't drink. I hope I never drink again. (Mind, I don't say, "I'll never drink again as long as I live." That might be sorta uncomfortable for me to live with.) How did I get down? How did I get up? I have heard from others a million sagas detailing the rationale — irrational in answer to the first of these two questions. They all differ and many are dramatic,

tragic, pathetic, frightening, sad — you name it. My own story fits in there somewhere. But, having succumbed to the ailment, its source or sources, though certainly academically important and worthy of pursuit, could for the time be shelved until rehabilitation has been consummated.

The beginning of my own resurrection was rather dramatic. I knew I had a drinking problem. I covered - or attempted to cover. I forgave those who subtly cajoled me to do this or do that. I kept my job. Much absence for illness. Lost too much weight. Wouldn't eat. Developed dietary, digestive, glandular troubles, high blood pressure, diabetes. At the time there didn't seem to be much point in changing my life pattern because the damage — physical, emotional, psychological — appeared inoperable. Might just as well live it up, die soon, and hopefully unaware of it all soaked in alcohol. I would have screamed 'Murder' had I thought that someone was attempting to enslave me; but I blindly set about enslaving myself to a bottle. Slave to a goddamn bottle!

There were so many other things I liked to do and ought to do. Things got worse. A vacation trip to the Rockies; stopped in a small provincial, red-necked town; charged with minor traffic violation; unconventional hair style, foreign-built car, out-of-state tags; sober; searched, manacled, arrested; charged with felony, possession of and transporting of marijuana; jailed three days and nights; mistreated, possessions impounded; newspaper publicity with pictures; national radio networks; F B eyed up to kazoo; Hoover cleaned; the younger set scurrying to the mountains for 'Silverweed' thinking it was grass; a tragicomedy of some moment produced at a cost of only 1 1/2 grand; completely cleared a month later; but the Oklahoma Bradleys disgraced by the oldest son.

Do you perchance remember an essay we studied in English Lit during your senior year at Harrah High School? The author: Alexander Pope; the subject: "Adversity." Its basic postulation was not really new and in earthy, less elegant language might say: after darkness comes the dawn; or every cloud has a silver lining; or

Things must get better 'cause they can't get any worse; or God works in wondrous ways; or Shit! Shit! enough is enough! Upon release on bond and in a sad mental and physical state, I retreated to Harmony House, a lovely alcohol and drug rehabilitation foundation in Estes Park, Colorado. Interesting people these addicts; wildflowers; birds; deer; abandoned mines; gold panning; park ranger; psychologists; swimming; cameras; rap sessions; folk songs and barber shop singing; leisurely reading; liquor available — coffee preferable; vitamins; wholesome food; Foundation president and staff all alcoholics; a millionaire Texas oil man; a penniless oil field roustabout; tall storied lies; laughter at our own weaknesses; self appraisal; sobriety. The end of a nightmare.

Tommy, I don't envision myself as a paragon of virtuosity, a showpiece for sobriety or any other such nonsensical image. There may be by-products of sobriety that enhance one's empathic approach to other people, but the golden fleece, the silver chalice, is mine. I no longer want to escape adversity. I want to meet it and beat it. Life is fun again. The family doctor is amazed at my vitality and general good health. He thinks he cured me. Maybe he did start the cure when he hinted that I might 'We' not be able to 'hack it' for very much longer. All of this became a undertaking. It was done with the love and understanding of Teddy, relatives, friends, and alcoholics.

We would love to hear from you. Better yet, come and see us. May I help you to the peaceful sleeping porch again?

Love, Bob

Oct. 14, 1997

Is a Generic Model of Recovery Possible?

By Scott N.

> *CThomas179@aol.com wrote: I read the Chapter to the Agnostic in the Big Book several times the other night. I was wondering about the AA approach, I kept reading it over and over, because I was amazed (don't know why) that they do say "just keep coming back, you'll get it, that so called spiritual experience".*

What is perhaps more amazing is that it does seem to happen to many people. Not that there is a genuine spiritual experience, but that many people believe they have had one after hanging around AA for a while.

Drawing on my own experience, I have some hypotheses about how it might come to pass. First, when I first sobered up, I had to deal with the fact that I drank and used during my entire adolescence and much of my twenties. As a result, I missed many of the experiences that mature and integrate a personality during those very important years. I was basically an empty shell of a person when it came time to sober up.

Secondly, I was in a hell of a lot of pain caused mostly by the emptiness and the shame of knowing what I was and how I got that way. I would have believed just about anything if I thought believing it would stop the pain and help me become a person. Then, here are all these people who described being like I had been, who seemed much better than I was who told me I could have what they had if I followed these few simple steps.

Looking back on it, I count myself lucky that I didn't fall into a more mind warping situation than AA. I was certainly vulnerable. At least they let me decide what HP I would choose. I would have ended up believing just about anything I heard repeated often enough.

I can't tell you how much anxiety I felt when I stopped attending meetings regularly. Turns out the quality of my sobriety improved considerably after I quit going.

In retrospect, I was being too open and honest, something else pounded into me. Yes it is possible to be, as a psychologist would put it, inappropriately self disclosing. I was shaming myself. The doubts, the fears, the desires, basically, all the dark side stuff. It turns out that at some point, it is important to put that stuff away and focus on the positive aspects of one's character, not just the parts that are problematic. I guess I had to grow out of AA to fully see that. For me at least, the AA personality I had put on when I got sober ended up being, while not empty, not my size either (not to mention the itchy cloth).

In a sense, many people who have been addicted need to change the way they view the world, and I mean a wholesale change. It is expedient for many of us to have a tailor made version to step into while we gèt our shit together. I now believe it does not have to be the AA version, though at one point I did. I find myself wondering if a generic model for recovery is possible. Most seem to agree on rule number one (i.e. abstinence). I wonder if there will ever be a second rule different camps pretty much agree on.

10/1/97

That Trip Out of Town

By Diane J., Mary Ann B., Craig M., and Hugh H.

Diane J. posted:

> *I have to attend a professional meeting this upcoming weekend, and I am looking for any suggestions people might have on successfully staying sober through it (anything from "Just don't drink!" to arcane rituals will be welcome). I'm sure you know the sticky parts: planes, trains, hotel bars, meeting cocktail hours, etc.*
> *Frankly, this has been something I haven't handled well before (why CAN'T that lady get into room 353? Right room number; ooops, wrong hotel, bye...) and I really intend to succeed this time.*
> *Any tips appreciated.*

Mary Ann replied:

Is there a meeting where you're going? Find out, plan to attend it. Skip the cocktail hour, if you have to go then go late (got caught up in work, networking etc...) have a soda, stay away from the bar and people who are obviously there for the drink. Better yet arrive late, bump into someone causing your drink to spill on you (wear light color, dark stainable juice) then you really must leave to change clothes and don't go back. Don't go into the hotel bar. Get a rental car (even if you have to pay for it), drive to a meeting (SOS, AA, NA, Alanon, Alateen). Tips on how to find a meeting: http://www.unhooked.com (SOS), phone book for AA, NA. Call the local treatment center/hosp. is there a meeting, or someone you can talk with. As for the airport, bring a SOS book, have the airport PA system page "any friend of J. Christopher or Bill W." to meet you for a mini meeting. Bring a sober friend with you to wait. Use the phone, call someone. Do airports have internet terminals now??? Sign on to SOS Email or Friends of Bill W. chat room. Hey, anything in a tempting situation is worth a try. Keep that last experience (oops, wrong hotel) fresh in your mind.

Craig replied:

I am off on a business trip this very week, and for the

first time in a while I was apprehensive about booze before I left — I was concerned that being in a small city in Montana at this time of year would be a problem, what with the early sundown and unavailability of the usual outdoor recreational options in this part of the country, as well as the omnipresence of bars in this frosty climate. Well, my concerns were unfounded, I have had absolutely no urge to throw away my life whatsoever. I even turned down repeated offers of beer and wine tonight when I had dinner at a colleague's home — and you know what? The antelope steaks were still yummy, the conversation was still amusing, and neither he nor his wife thought any less of me because I chose not to drink. I had a really good time, and I know that I behaved well enough that they meant it when they said they wanted to see me again. It's a good feeling.

You don't have to drink to have fun. You don't have to drink to be interesting. There are only two possible reasons to drink: because you want to or because you need to. Since you are here, it is pretty clear that you don't really want to. And since you are here, you have probably decided that you need not to drink more than you need to drink. So just keep in mind that no matter what, there is no possible reason that you should pick up a bottle, regardless of what others (be they "normal" or drunks like us) do.

Hugh replied:

Diane and all, I haven't joined in the discussion till now; I've just been eavesdropping, but I appreciate this problem, Diane. I'm a historian and these conferences are REALLY tough tests of sobriety. What I've done is just flat out tell people I have stopped drinking because too often in the past I have gotten knee-walking and I don't want to chance that any more. The reaction has been almost uniformly favorable: people were GLAD AND RELIEVED that I would not be making an obnoxious spectacle of myself. People who didn't know me, didn't care that I didn't drink. And what a difference it made! Instead of returning home with an aching head and fervent hopes that I was not wanted by the local police, I had lots of new, useful information for lectures, etc. and, more important, clear memories of good times with old friends I only get to see at these conferences. I really can't imagine screwing up one of these occasions again for the sake of alcohol. I really enjoy this group and have benefited from it enormously.

Diane responded:

I just wanted to thank you all for the very useful and creative suggestions and support. It has been definitely helpful for me to see how other people handle this kind of situation. I've printed all of your e-mails and will be taking them with me this evening.

I also used your suggestions in combination with a technique in the SOS Handbook. I sat down last night and listed off all of the potential PROBLEM situations I could imagine arising and then matched them with possible SOLUTIONS:

"Liking those little bottles of California Chardonnay on the plane" — make sure I have something nonalcoholic to drink.

"Going out with a group of former colleagues" — try just telling them that I stopped drinking — they'll probably be just as glad; remember that there is no reason for me to pick up a bottle...et cetera.

I realize that this might sound like major overkill (I even called the hotel to make sure the room doesn't have a minibar!), but this is the first time I have traveled for any reason and I want it to be a success.

Three days later, Diane posted:

Hi!

I just wanted to thank everyone for all of the advice and support re: conference travel. It WORKED! Had a very nice time (actually remember the content of the sessions! -- laugh), enjoyed seeing old colleagues — and even attended two receptions fueled by nothing stronger than Diet Coke. (I did skip the invitation to go "brewpub crawling", however -- went back to my hotel and got into the pool instead, then went down for a nice dinner with a good book. I brought all your e-mail with me and it was most helpful to review the suggestions and my plan and to know that I HAD a plan, and options to deal with it.

Didn't even want to drink on the train ride home -- AND

got an unexpected bonus from that: turned out my boss was on the same train (unrelated travel) and we didn't know it till we disembarked (by which time yours truly USUALLY would have had at least three of those cunning little bottles of wine ("oh, they're SO small....").

Anyway, thank you all once again, and enjoy a sober Tuesday! (Even if it IS cloudy and Novembery here, it's not cloudy in my head today. And it doesn't have to be anymore.

Diane

Nov. 5 - 11, 1997

We Can More Freely Tell

By Ben B.

This is an important idea that I couldn't talk about in AA, that we don't all have the same experiences.

When I was six months sober my AA sponsor was talking about blackouts. When I said I rarely had blackouts, he said in a patronizing way "keep coming back." The idea in AA is that because we're all "alcoholics," we all have all the "symptoms" of "alcoholism," so my sponsor thought I must have had many blackouts, and I was just in denial about it. The truth is that our (not just the people on this list, or in SOS, but all people who have drinking problems) drinking patterns were often very different. Many people regularly had blackouts caused by drinking, but certainly not all. Some people got drunk from the first time they drank, and always got drunk when they drank. Others had years of drinking in which they only had one or two drinks at a time. Some got DUIs, some didn't. Some never drove drunk. And on and on...

I like this about the SOS list: that we can more freely tell what we were really like, without having to have done any one thing or combination of things ('symptoms') while drinking to 'qualify' us to be here. I still see (dare I say it...) a little group-think here, but it's a vast improvement over where I spent my early sobriety...

11/14/97

Change the Behavior Now!

By Ron C.

Eric wrote:

Today is 60 days for me! It's been interesting, every day is a learning experience. Eric :-)

Eric,

This recovery process isn't one gradual continuum of felt progress.

My actions and values, especially those I eventually changed in sobriety, were acutely operative in early sobriety.

All of the feelings about myself (usually negative) and all of my learned methods of dealing with the world (usually inappropriate and self-defeating) continued into sobriety.

It is.....the very fact that "every days is a learning experience" that allows me to evaluate and to change my method of living. "That" learning now reinforces my sobriety.

If you notice the emergence of a behavior that you know contributes to your drinking, CHANGE the behavior NOW. That's what learning is all about.

If you notice the emergence of feelings about yourself that contribute to your drinking, CHANGE the feelings Now.....you learned to feel that way and you will learn to feel other ways.

I continually remind myself that "the action does not determine the response, I determine the response."

Such is what makes the Sobriety Priority work.....such is what make me responsible for my sobriety and my life..... such is what makes life wonderful, interesting and most curious.

11/24/97

Ixnay Eagles

By Jim S., Barbara A., Ben B., Larry D., Scott N., and Jim S.

Jim S. asked for advice:

OK, friends, I have a serious dilemma and will pose it thus. I've been invited to travel to Philadelphia Sunday for an Eagles game. I am so damn new in this sobriety business that I'm questioning whether I should attend or not. $60 free tickets. One of my dreams has been to attend a pro football game. I had the good fortune of attending a Pirates game in a private box (again, free of charge) last summer and had a blast. I was drinking but still tremendously enjoyed it. [...] I (if I go) will be traveling with a drinker. I have considered being the Des Driver.

Even my wife is pushing me to go with the logic that I didn't get sober to sit around with my thumb up my a_ _. It rather shocked me that she mentioned if I slip I can always start over again when I get back Sunday night. That tells me she has not a clue as to the scope of this most insidious problem. I can't fault her for that since she is not and never will be an alcoholic.

We are a group of people who know what it is to be there. I certainly don't want her blessing to drink and would just like some simple suggestions to stay clean at this early place in my recovery. Something someone said on this list is beginning to sink in to this feeble mind. I will give proper credit to whoever it was since you know who you are even if I forgot. "I want to not want to drink." That is where I am at this time. Can I sustain this thinking? Any and all suggestions will be very much appreciated, taken to heart, written down, read and re-read; hell I'll even eat the notes if it will help. Thank you all for taking time to read this.

Barbara A. answered:

Hello Jim, Everyone.

I'm not usually one to give advice, but since you have asked... I'm not a sports fan, maybe because I'm not eating my quota of 1.5 inch steaks, and I'm trying to imagine an equivalent thrill for me that would include a possible return to drinking ....hummm ...hummm. Well, I'll keep working on that. Anyway, when I was first new at not drinking, finding it hard, the AA advice (see, Ben I have remembered to quote my sources) was — if you don't want to slip, don't go where it's slippery. I could pick some holes in that one now, but the basic message still rings true for me. Slippery for me is not so much an environment now, but a state of mind, but it hasn't always been like that.

Why voluntarily put yourself in an uncomfortable, possibly unsafe position, that may lead back to drinking ?

Answers come to mind as — the possible risk is worth the possible reward — or you're making plans to drink again. I really steered away from those "slippery places" when I was under pressure. You seem under pressure to me, Jim — another very new sobriety, work overload, holiday season, wife who won't be too upset if you do drink again, what else...? How much fun will it be to go to that game if you do drink ? How much fun will it be to avoid the game because it may be a risk to your new attempt at sobriety? You are young, more good offers will come your way.

Ben B. answered:

It's certainly true that we don't get sober to live a boring life and never get out to have fun, but you appear to lack confidence that you can stay sober through this event. If you choose not to go, what would be an alternative? Try figuring out how much you spent on alcoholic beverages (and don't even count possible peripheral expenses such as increased risk of car damage or a DUI assuming you drove drunk, or more intangible expenses such as reduced job performance/ attendance and strained personal relationships). Figure out how long it would have taken you to spend $60. Maybe a month? Now, when does the football season end? If the season ends before you save up $60 that you would have spent on drinking, then how about next year? Will the Eagles play again in Philadelphia? I've heard about these football teams relocating. (Are the Eagles the Philadelphia team? I'm not much of a sports fan myself) The Falcons have been in Atlanta for 30 years — I happen to hear the sports whenever I watch the TV news, and the Falcons are (ahem) not going anywhere. Again, I've never been a fan and never been to a Pro Football game — perhaps the Falcons are why :-) I think you get the idea — one of the rewards of sobriety can be doing something you've always wanted to do, even if you have to pay for it yourself. If you plan to go to a later game when you'll feel more confident, you'll have time to find another sober fan to go with you.

You posted: "I want to not want to drink. That is where I am at this time. Can I sustain this thinking?"

Only you can actually answer that, but it would certainly be easier at a later time in sobriety.

Larry D. responded:

Hi Jim, I've really enjoyed your accounts of your early days a lot, and I'll take this chance to say something back, and add to what Barb and Ben have already offered. As much as we are pulling for you, I don't think many people on this list would feel comfortable trying to tell you what you have to do to stay sober. For better or worse, the SOS program forces each of us to apply the sobriety priority to our individual situation and personality — whatever it takes is what it takes for you to stay sober, not for me. If for you that means football games, then don't look back, it's bye-bye Eagles. For now, anyway. But if that doesn't include football for you, then Go Eagles! That kind of freedom can be a great to a person who has some sober experience, but I can see where it might be a little overwhelming to somebody new to the game.

Although you don't have to swear off football for the rest of your life, would it make good sense to take a rain check on this one? If it was me, I think a lot of my decision would hinge on the friend I would be going with. If he was a person who already knew I was not drinking, and I knew that he would support me in that even if he was drinking himself, I might not feel too vulnerable. But if I haven't felt comfortable sharing my decision with him and would be faced on my own with a whole host of subtle pressures to drink, I would figure I would either succumb or be miserable, and I would avoid the situation like the plague. And treat myself to the biggest consolation prize I could think of, to ease my temptation to feel sorry for myself. I've never been to a pro football game in my life, so it would be really easy for me to say no. Maybe to you it is more of a once-in-a lifetime thing, and to pass it up would make you feel really deprived.

Of course, if you knew for sure, or even thought there was a pretty good chance that you would drink, your decision would be an easy one. You have a lot invested already in those thirteen sober days, and as you pointed out, your wife's reassurance that you can always quit again, however well meaning it was, just doesn't make any sense in light of that investment. Not only does staying sober get easier with time, our increasing investment in sober time also makes it easier and easier to convince ourselves not to throw it away and have to start all over again. I remember saying to myself many, many times "I sure don't want to have to go through that again!" And I never did have to, once I quit for good.

Reading over what I just wrote, I sound even to myself like a big mugwump, but I don't think I can do any better. Anyway you slice it, it is your call. The sobriety priority can guide you, but you will find a lot of different translations of that principle even among our group. Good luck to you!

Scott N. posted:

I don't know what will work for you, but when I gave up drinking and drugging 10+ years ago, I also quit hanging around others who drink and drug. That was necessary for me at the time to stay sober. I also changed jobs and professions because the stresses and temptations of my old life were a threat that I chose not to dance with. I also moved 30 miles down the road, went into treatment, served 2 years probation rather than a quick 30 days in county that was offered by the judge. I could go on, but my point is that I had to do what I had to do to stay sober. Sobriety was my first priority and in order to keep it, I knew I had to be willing to give up anything that would seriously jeopardize that priority. What I found out is that through giving up my old life so completely, room was made for me to start a new one that was and continues to be enormously more rewarding. I have paid to see both Astros games and Rangers games in the past two years and enjoyed them intensely. Went with my sober wife and son. Hope this helps.

Jim S. responded:

Well, I decided to not go to the Eagles game Sunday. I thought very long and hard about what you all wrote and of course you're right. Why chance a slip on a slippery slope? I told my wife of my decision and to say she was ecstatic would be an understatement. She mentioned how "nice" I've been these last couple weeks and would hate to see me blow it. After all the bullshit I've put her through these last years she has every right to be selfish yet she is not. I can in fact watch on TV and quaff a few diet Squirts. Funny, I was thinking about one of my 3 older brothers the other day who is nonalcoholic (as are the other 2) and he used to ask me rather nastily if I was that thirsty would I be drinking a 12 pack of Pepsi? I think not. I didn't lie to the gentleman who invited me but told him politely that something important had come up that I had forgotten about and could I take a rain check. No problemo. I do not feel deprived in the least as I did feel uncomfortable enough to ask for advice. In the past that would not have happened — trust me on that one.

I used a model I found in my desk drawer this morning. On one side the blank section had possible benefits of drinking and on the opposite the possible problems or risks involved. Guess which side had the most writing in it? […]

Thanks for the support friends....it's what I needed, when I most needed it. I really didn't expect to be confronted with this dilemma in the first place. Some people take my gregarious and outgoing nature behind the counter to be the "real" me. I'm a very good actor. I guess you could call that a very important retail skill. I've been offered jobs as sales director, stock broker, you name it. I tell people that I just can't lie <G>. Like hell, I've lied so much during the drinking that the truth became nonexistent. I'm getting better though. Even my employees have noticed a big change in me in this most early stage. They like it better. A sober Jim beats a poke in the eye with a sharp stick any day!

Best to you all this fine evening. Tomorrow is Thanksgiving Eve and I will lovingly wrap all your hearts safely in bubble paper and give thanks for what I've received from my new friends.

11/24-11/26/97

Thirty Days Sober And What Do You Get?

By Jim S.

Thirty days and what did I get?
I found my self-respect, so long lacking.
I found my business again and am enjoying it.
I found people no longer antagonize me.
I found money in my pockets.
I found much, much, more time on my hands.
I found my real friends are still my real friends.
I found my "alcohol abuser" friends are still alcohol abusers.
I found myself jumping out of bed full of enthusiasm.
I found my employees talking to me about important life matters.
I found I'm a very productive person.
I found the beauty of books once again.
I found I'm not nearly as stupid as I look.
I found that not everyone pukes daily.
I found chocolate.
I found dinner to be special with my family.
I found that my wife does/did not hate me ... just the booze.
I found my kids really do love their dad in spite of my faults and foibles.
I found I can be there for them.
I found my paranoia was unfounded.
I found poetry.
I found creative writing.
I found how to fix things heretofore impossible.
I found comedy to be funny.
I found the people in my wife's church are not all hypocrites.
I found Christmas shopping to be a joy rather than a burden.
I found the damn cats like me sober.
I found strength in numbers.
I found happiness and peace.
I found no pink cloud, just honest to goodness sobriety.

I found I need not project nor forecast the future.

I found (from Pigpen in Charlie Brown's Christmas) "Frankly, I didn't think I looked this good."

I found tolerance of others views.

I found I'm not always right.

I found others are not always right either.

I found there are some very good people in this world.

I found there likewise to be a not-so-short supply of evil.

I found I can enjoy life rather than merely survive it.

I found you folks.

I found some great slice of strength you all seem to possess and exhibit.

I found I never announced anniversaries in AA, as I tended to look to the future with the attitude (or maybe I just never "got it") that most seemed to treat their time "clean" as time "deprived". I don't want to fall into that trap again.

You get bit the first time it's the dogs fault, the second time its your own fault.

Love and friendship to all you fine people.

I don't think, or maybe I do, that this is the first month of the rest of my life.

Chaos bless, God bless, Buddha bless, Zoroaster bless, Great Spirit bless, oh and lets not forget Jean Dixon!

Jim

12/8/97

Haiku

By MOG

I look out my window to the southeast on Long Island's far point.
The dark turns to a wide band of red, then apricot.
A herring gull sits in the osprey nest.
He also didn't drink last night.

12/29/97

Reach Out and Touch

By Jane D.

Spent my Xmas with family -- some of my most dangerous buttons. Got through it. And it really was OK. The same old conflicts, a bunch of new ones. I didn't drink and didn't have much problem with it then even though this is the first holiday season I can remember (literally) having been sober.

So, I'm on Amtrak coming home and I'm not sure whether or not it was that the relief of getting through the holidays wasn't coming fast enough to suit me or whether it was that I was feeling the need for a reward or boredom or what, but my lizard mind started rationalizing. One glass of wine wouldn't hurt. After all, I didn't drink when my buttons were pushed; when the pressure was on, so one glass of wine couldn't hurt now. My seat was less than one car down from the club car. That made it very convenient.

The power went off. They had to get a diesel to push us to a new power line. But the power was only enough to run the engine -- no heat or lights. A three hour trip took me six-plus hours. As the hours grew, and, as I couldn't smoke on the train, my lizard got stronger. The line to the Club Car got long. As they passed me, I noticed a very young, very harassed mom with baby and started to talk. I offered to get her what she needed so she could sit down with cranky babe in tow. She took me up on it. I got on that line still debating on getting my booze and wanting it real bad by that time. Bought two waters, walked extra cars to find and give it to her. Took the baby in my arms and walked her for an hour or so up and down the aisle; her under my coat to try and give her some warmth in the cold.

As I walked her, that small child reminded me how precious life is; mine included.

That was my small holiday miracle. Happy New Year!

12/31/97

Smirnoff Memories

By Craig M.

Marty wrote: We've been going to movies on this vacation. Just saw the new Bond flick, something about Tomorrow. There's a scene where he's waiting for an ex-flame to show up at his hotel room for a very delicate negotiation with possible sex and he's priming himself by drinking double shots of Smirnoff out of a shot glass. By the time she arrives he's had three doubles that we've seen, who knows how many before that. This scene is nothing but a commercial for Smirnoff. If you liked vodka this has high trigger potential, so watch out.

Smirnoff Vodka... the memories. The sweet burning taste of 100 proof vodka pouring straight from the bottle down my throat until it hit my stomach and made me subtly jerk forward with what remained of my gag reflex. A backpack smuggling the pint bottle with the blue label every time I entered or left the house. Only buying pints because each would be the last (for at least a while), but doing this at least once a day. Eating breakfast primarily because it meant avoiding the pain of the dry heaves when I puked in the bushes in the Berkeley Rose Garden on my way to campus. Not being able to get the right high anymore no matter how much I drank, figuring out that I had reached a point where there was no pleasure left in the bottle, and then continuing to drink nonstop for months anyway. Being freed at crucial times of silly self-imposed constraints like manners and respect, thus enabling me to really do my share in the downward spiral of my marriage.

Smirnoff memories, they might trigger another 3 years of sobriety.

Craig M.

1/6/98

A Secret Shame

by Marianne H.

SOS friends:

We had a thread a while back about how open to be about being alcoholic. I was one who didn't want to tell anybody, and it seemed some other recently sober folks felt the same way. Many folks with more sober time felt that selective informing made sense, and others advocated shouting from the rooftops.

After chewing on all the different ideas in that thread, I decided there was one person I had to tell—the woman who had been my role model for nearly 20 years, and who had cared enough to threaten to deny me contract work if I didn't stop drinking, then did just that when nothing changed.

Obviously, she knew I drank to excess. So it wasn't sharing a nasty secret that I was avoiding with her. I think I was afraid to tell her I'd quit drinking for fear I'd blow it. SOS has since taught me that (a) there's no shame in being an alcoholic, particularly a former one, (b) honesty in appropriate situations makes life easier, and (b) if I should blow it, I could just start over to be sober again without its being the end of the world.

Those three notions have taken much pressure off me. Enough that today I sent my role model friend e-mail thanking her for her tough love, and in what way it had helped. Her response came within the hour and said, in part, "WOW! This is terrific news. I am happy for you. It is an admirable journey you have embarked upon and, I understand, not an easy one. I can only be a distant cheerleader, but count me in."

There are many SOSers now with even less sober time than I, and maybe some are feeling as uncertain as I did about whether and how to share the decision not to drink. If so, perhaps this will help

1/30/98

Diversity Begets Hope

By Roger K.

What I discern as a shared value in SOS is sobriety, not the means to get there, though SOS seems to value pragmatic discourse about what works for various individuals. This diversity of answers begets hope. I am not alone. Others are fighting my fight, and they share what works, without having to posit closed universes of methods, steps, higher powers, or whatever. This takes me out of the corner that I painted myself into with alcohol. Furthermore, I get to share what works for me without suffering the flames and arrows of those who posit singular dogmatic solutions. We each own our individual, possibly dogmatic solution and recognize the validity of other answers without requiring that the answer be valid for all. We don't have to suspend disbelief, pick up a cross, or any particular other thing. What we have to do is not drink today, no matter what.

I feel better now. Whoever's next, the soapbox is yours.

1/26/98

Drinking "At"

By CA, Marianne H., Laura L., Marty N., Carol H.

CA began it:

… I couldn't sleep because I thought I was going to have to suspend a student, and ended up drinking. …

Marianne replied:

… Hope that next time someone gets in a jam, you won't punish yourself because of it…

CA responded:

I never thought of it as punishing myself, but maybe that's what I was doing. You've helped me see this in a new way.

Laura joined in:

I had a counselor who referred to this "phenomenon" as "Drinking AT somebody." During the time(s) when I was lapsing like that, it became very important to me to understand the connection between anger, sadness and shame in my own life. Among others, I drank "at" a staff member who was ultimately terminated. I had given her every chance, encouragement, training, threat, cajoling, etc. I was angry that she was "doing this TO ME." I was sad because I knew, eventually she'd be let go, and I was ashamed because I felt that the failure was mine. I drank at other people too, but she really sticks in my mind for some reason; probably because of the fallacious argument within my own mind, and the faulty logic I used to make myself feel even worse. Hope this makes some kind of sense.

Marty chimed in:

Thank you for that expression, Laura. It really fits. I used to do it all the time.

Marianne responded:

Me, too. My prime client paid me up to $650/day, so I thought I couldn't justify turning down the work. However, we did not share the same values, so our relationship over the years was uneasy, at best, and unbearable at worst. So I drank *at* the organization, and particularly at whichever person represented its side of our latest dysfunctional interaction. Did that for nearly nine years, although nothing changed except I dug myself a deeper and deeper hole.

When I quit drinking in November, I began to think more clearly about that working relationship. And decided to wind it down as quickly and as gracefully as I could. To wind it down, "no matter what," to coin a phrase, and even though I had no idea where to find replacement income. The day early in January when I mailed my last invoice was, tellingly, the first day I *knew* I could stay sober. I wouldn't need to drink *at* my so-called "friends" any more.

Of, course, that wasn't the only reason I drank. But it was sure a biggie, and it's nice to have the phrase "drinking at" to remind me that I mustn't get into that ever again.

Carol picked it up:

... Yesterday, I got angry with a friend and the first thing I thought of was having a beer. And then I remembered that someone on the list had said "I had a counselor who referred to this "phenomenon" as "Drinking AT somebody." That helped me and for once I didn't partake of my old friend.

Thanks again.

And CA closed the circle:

Tonight I'm trying Being Sober AT My Students. In other words, I want to be refreshed and clear for them tomorrow.

1/29-2/8/98

A Hard Note to Write

by MOG

Fellow SOS Strivers,

This is a hard note to write but hopefully helpful to myself and perhaps others.

Emotional interrelational problems began to surface last Thursday for me and someone I care for. I went back to smoking. Friday was not a good day. Saturday, when my failure to resolve the difficulties became debilitating and apparently hopeless (I became obsessed with solution), I crossed the line.

Some part of my being slipped into old thoughts of despair and the pain in my chest became more intense. I bought three large bottles of French Wine and came home and sat looking out at Goose Creek turning the pages of a book on Anger (since that seemed to be the center of the problem). Almost immediately I called a fellow SOS person near here and emailed a close friend in SOS.

Details of the day include some grasp of my reasons for drinking (I overreacted to another person with obsession, I had not solved some rather major emotional problems, I did not call anyone before I drank--I just wanted relief, I did not take other people into consideration, and I took the easy way out) and my own proclivity to use alcohol as a solution for problems that such action would not solve.

I was fortunate that the offended person called, provided herself with an outlet for the anger that she felt, and led me to the idea of therapy. I received help from the SOS list, and my friend came by, talked, and went off with the remaining two bottles of wine.

I wanted no more wine. Sunday the woman called and we met in the afternoon with much better aspects and with definite plans for therapy.

I was fortunate in stopping quickly and now must work at the emotional problems and strengthen my attitudes toward abstinence. I realized that the almost two years of sobriety that I had was very helpful. I had partially faced some of the emotional problems while sober, I had built up a number of very positive attitudes towards abstinence and its pleasures, joys, and aid in solving difficulties, and I had a bank of self esteem that I could eventually tap.

I am fragile today but resolved again in not drinking. In many ways, this slip has fired me to face some of my misaligned thoughts and now I move forward, taking steps slowly and one at a time.

I fortunately feel no shame nor guilt but do see the hard hold that alcohol can take on someone and realize that movement to abstinence is a huge struggle for many of us.

Best, MOG

13 Apr 98

The Look On His Face

By Lynne L.

Hi all,

I wanted to thank everyone (Marty, Barbara, Shirl, Mary-Ann, and Diane) for the support and responses. My cravings seem to have subsided. It's nice to know I can get thru them without picking up and that many other people have too. I hate when my brain goes back into its addictive thinking mode. At least I can identify how distorted my thinking is. I also need to put into my toolbox the bad memories associated with my drug use. If I can remember the night I had to call my parents to bail me out of jail (at age 33 no less and $5 short of the bail) because I had a blackout or seizure while driving as a result of abrupt withdrawal of benzodiazepines (xanax and valium) and caused an accident at a rotary. Of course, how I got there is a whole different story. I have no memory of it and have never been to that part of Cape Cod. I was lucky. No one was injured. I don't ever want that to happen again. If I can remember that, hopefully I won't pick up.

On the brighter side, I will be going to see my 3 year old and 2 week old nephews tomorrow. Being with them always makes my day. Of course, I'll be taking the 3 year old to see the Barney movie. Thank goodness it's only 75 minutes long. But it's worth it to see the look on his face when "Aunti Lynne" gets there. That look helps me to stay sober. I want to be able to see that look for many more years. If I started using again, I wouldn't be able to see his beautiful face and see his younger brother grow up with him.

(Aunti) Lynne

8 Apr 1998

The Credit is Mine

By Shirley B.

I'm here because (1) I had to get out of AA after 3 mos. My self-esteem on entering was at a new low point and they were going to take the rest of it. I wanted credit for getting and staying sober and I wasn't going to pass it over to them. The thought of a "sponsor" (and a total stranger) telling me how to run my life and point out my character "defects" was the final touch. (Hell, I still have my mother for that.)

And (2) This town has only AA. I think the nearest SOS to me is probably MOG's in Long Island. But I am considering starting one here. I have the sober time to do it now. There has to be other sober alcoholics in AA that would love to leave just like the rest of us. So for now I stay sober on my own, with lots of encouragement from friends on this list, but I take the glory!

Shirl

4/9/98

I Want a Life Much More Than I Want a Drink

By Diane J.

> *L. wrote: I can really relate to this thread. At 5:30 pm I celebrated 5 months. Not bad for the first time in over 10 years of daily drugging. I wasn't having a big problem with craving until about 2 weeks ago. Now I'm going nuts.*

Hi!

First, congratulations on the five months and it's nice to hear from another five-monther here (I'm five months and ten days, personally). And let me throw in some hearty commiseration. I've been "going nuts" craving for a solid week myself, after a couple of months of mostly perfect good cheer and lack of strong craving. Last week it kicked in: constant thoughts of drinking (my drug was vodka, with the occasional bottle or two of wine for variation), drunk dreams, EXACTLY and PRECISELY the kind of "logical" thinking (hey, no problem, time for a little relapse, plenty of people do THAT, right?) that you describe.

A specialist friend of mine tells me that 5-7 months sober is often a time of renewed craving, in his observation. You feel better physically, the memories of how bad it got (i.e., why you got desperate enough to stop in the first place) dim a little, you get tired of how much WORK sobriety seems to be and how many changes it seems to require in your life..... Maybe some of that applies for you, too? I thought it might help to hear that it doesn't seem to be that unusual a problem for us addicts.

What helps me not pick up is, when it's at its worst, keeping the memories dusted off. I don't dwell on it, but sometimes I need to not-so-gently remind myself that I've heard that logic in my head before, and I ran right after it, it was so beautifully plausible. I damn near didn't survive in one piece to "get sober again." I'm glad there are people who have "repeater's luck," but any thought that I'm one of them is a dangerous fantasy.

Also, I remind myself that I've DONE that---and I'm sick of it. I'm tired of drinking/not drinking eating up so much of my life: alcohol can't be worth the amount of intelligence and passion and effort I've devoted to it. I want to USE all of that for something else. And if sitting through craving for a while is the first step, I'll sit.

> *The only thing that got me thru this weekend was the free HBO and Cinemax on cable. I ended up watching a ton of movies which I found distracted me from my cravings.*

I envy you this one, I really do. Television is a trigger for me, unfortunately. I can barely watch anything without an impulse to pick up a bottle of vodka. (Umm...that even includes the Moyers special last week (laugh). Saw that lovely close up of shelves FULL of Majorska bottles and thought, "gee, yeah, why the hell not" — which is an odd thing to be thinking.)

I try to find enjoyable distractions — reading works for me — some addiction-related, some not. Going for walks works. Sitting quietly outside on a nice day and reminding myself that feeling this good and calm and pleased with the sun and the breeze and being in my own skin is NOT compatible with getting drunk. And I WANT this feeling. And I'm curious. I can see the progress, even in the craving, over the past months. I want to see what MORE and LONGER will be like for me.

I want a life. Much more than I want a drink.

Hope this helps some and congratulations on getting this far.

Take care,
Diane J.

8 Apr 1998

And a month later:

> *L. wrote: Tomorrow will be 6 months for me. This is the first time in my life I've tried to get clean. Yeah for me and my program. It works.*

Hip hip hooray from me too. And, BTW, I hit 6 MONTHS myself earlier this week. I'm astonished--that's the longest I've been sober in a quarter of a century!

Thank you, ALL of you, for being here! I had almost absolutely NO hope that this would work when I finally came off a rough long mostly self-detox at the end of October, except for the encouraging words from the detox doctor I finally called when I got too sick to move ("Ummm....yeah, you can do it that way, but why don't you let me take a look at you and make sure you're not going to kill yourself in the process"... listened patiently to my rant about how I wasn't going NEAR anything that LOOKED like AA and about how I wasn't going NEAR anything that looked like my previous experience with 'treatment', and then said the magic words:

"Hey, you know, people get sober without AA all the time. Why not give it a shot? You don't sound like you're having much of a good time drinking any more."

Onward to another six months!!

Thank you all.

Diane J.

("Hey, I'm an alcoholic--it's not like I'm powerless or anything.")

7 May 1998

Sober Mother's Days

by Shirley B. and Nancy K.

Shirley wrote: Wishing all our sober mothers a happy Mother's Day! What are little girls made of? They're made of sugar and spice and everything nice.

I'm lucky today to have sleeping in the next room my oldest daughter and my granddaughter who arrived around midnight. Last year I would have been dragging myself out of bed to greet them, but this year I was up and functioning. We watched Anastasia together and fell asleep. I'm up early with no headache, no sick feelings, no vodka in the orange juice. I'll be able to fix a nice breakfast and have fun doing it. I'll have patience with my granddaughter and won't care if she runs through the house, says NO fifty times, and doesn't want to sit down and eat. I won't end up criticizing my daughter for ANYTHING. There isn't any bottle of anything that is going to spoil this for us.

Hope everyone has a good day :).

Shirl

Nancy K. responded:

Hey Shirl!

Happy, CLEAN AND SOBER Mothers' Day to you, I am envious that you have yours with you today. Mine are in the NC mountains living and loving life. "We celebrate Mother's day everyday" is how they view this "Hallmark" day. I am a "clean and sober" Mom, and nothing is better than this! I am off to "mother" all of my horses, dogs, and cats. Animals and nature are my greatest sources of strength in life, I am so fortunate to be living among and with … a path I was able to follow by getting and living sober.

If I can do it … ANYONE can!

Later, Nancy

10 May 1998

Zealotry is Itself an Addiction

by Dave W.

The need for many people to cleave to AA as their "only hope to stay sober" does not surprise me. I sometimes think that religious zealotry is itself an addiction — being drunk on the love and forgiveness of God to numb the pain and loneliness we feel in our emotionally arrested lives. Ironically, it seems that our need to medicate the shame and hopelessness in our lives was created by the underlying premise of a supernatural being creating our world, dictating our absolute morality, and judging our unworthiness to exist for eternity.

Posted 5/18/98

No, No, I Don't! Cancel That!

by Alice I.

My husband, daughter and I arrived in Ft. Myers FL on Saturday at 3:30 PM. After 20 minutes in the car with my parents I knew that there was no way I would make it through these 5 days with no alcohol. I decided to throw in the towel and start all over upon arrival home.

We went to their house where dad announced to me that he had gotten me beer, it was in the fridge. (This was no big deal, I knew there would be alcohol everywhere. I had not told them that I had stopped drinking, they never really cared when I had before.) I avoided the lurking fridge-dwellers for the time until we left for dinner.

At dinner my father asked, "Alice, you want a beer?" I quickly and confidently replied "yes." The look my husband shot me was like cold water in my face. Immediately I thought "No! no I don't! Cancel that!" I said nothing. The Miller Lite (my water-beer of choice) arrived as requested. It loomed there before me. By now I knew this was wrong. I REALLY did not want it.

I poured about half into the chilled glass. Waited. Took a sip. It tasted good. I took another. It did not taste good. I guzzled the glass of water and asked for more water. I ended up nursing that beer until half of it was gone. By that time I had had seven 10 ounce glasses of water. I had no buzz (imagine that). I had to pee twice, though.

I never got "high," never wanted to finish the last half of the beer. I did not have another drink for the entire trip and I do not want or need a drink now. Instead, for the next 72 hours I was never caught without a glass of water in my hand. I was asked again if I wanted beer, but declined. MUCH TO THE CHAGRIN OF MY VERY ALCOHOLIC FATHER! BOY WAS HE MAD! I guess he prefers me drunk when he is drunk ...which is always.

I am trying not to look on this as a failure, but as a stepping stone. My parents drank in front of me and were pretty blasted the whole time I was there. This is not new, but SEEING it through CLEAR eyes was. It was horrible. Not the sobriety, but to see people do that to themselves. My parents and I have never been close (although they like to think we are). I almost threw in the towel. But I have come so far, I won't give up now.

5/22/98

Survival In the Air

By Carolyn, Bob, Alice, Leigh, Mark, Marianne & Carol

I have been on vacation in Gulfport and everything has been going good. I've had no urges to drink, etc., even while in the casino. But when thinking of returning to Florida, the thoughts hit me about drinking when I get on the airplane, etc. I've been trying to think them through but I am concerned.

Any advice??

Carolyn

Just don't, no matter what!

Bob

Try this! When you get on the plane put all your cash in the bottom of a carry-on bag and stash it in the back of an overhead bin that is about three rows away!!

When the stewards come by, the inconvenience should overcome the urge to purchase something.

Alice :)

What a great idea! Or better yet, put your cash in with the baggage that you checked. Then you'll really be inconvenienced! Sometimes I keep sweets in the trunk of my car rather than in my apartment because once I get started on them, bringing the whole container to the table to eat is very easy, but if I have to go get them out of the car, it doesn't seem worth the effort.

Leigh

Carolyn, bring a really good book to read during the flight. (I couldn't read when I was drinking). Call somebody right before your flight. Got any AA or SOS reading material with you? You could read that on the plane. Keep talking it through in your head. You know where drinking gets you. Think the drink through. Everyone in the group is waiting for you to return sober and healthy...and richer???? Call me if you need to talk.

Mark

Carol, carry bottled water with you. One more bottle than you think you'll need. Flavored, if your prefer. Treat yourself to one of those insulated lunch box bags and bum a Ziploc bag to put ice cubes in so you can keep the small bottles cold. Don't know how you feel about soft drinks, but ask for two glassfuls at a time -- they don't come by all that often these days!

--Marianne

I really liked the responses I got, I thought about what Alice wrote about, putting my money somewhere else. It kind of took me when I read that, because I was amazed that I hadn't thought of that myself. I guess that's why everyone is here on the list. I took a newspaper on the plane with me and thought about how miserable it would be if I had a drink because I would be riding in a "shared limo," knowing that I couldn't "have another one" until I got home. Could you image riding with a bunch of strangers for a hour or two, right after having just "one" beer. That would be torture. Anyway, had a diet coke and enjoyed talking to a young girl beside me. She was from New Orleans and told me she had been shot at the age of 14 from a drive by. We were talking about the crime rate there.

I also made a little over $400.00.

See everyone Friday night in St. Pete

Carolyn

Carolyn, All: I too, want to thank everyone as I am going on a flight in a few weeks and had been wondering the same thing as Carolyn. I'm glad she asked and also glad for the responses. I shall print out the responses and keep them for when I have to fly. (I hate flying.)

Carol

5/22-5/27/98

I Sure Don't Fit the Mold

By John A.

[Michael H. posted: My personal best was listing 12 step meetings as a relapse trigger the last time I was in treatment. My counselor just couldn't seem to get her mind around that concept.]

Dear Michael and all SOSers: My journey in AA and SOS has been anything but normal. I had a sponsor back in '72 who was a hard core atheist. He thought the world of AA but could not get the god concept. He died sober with over 30 years sobriety. He had met the founders and was a very fine man.

There was another man, named Tom D. He is dead now so I can tell the story. He used to be at the AA meetings and was the first AAer who had a coin. He had a silver dollar with holes drilled in it. He had over 20 years sobriety, and that was in '72-'73.

He was a dedicated AAer who was a bible thumper and god fear man. He came off skid row. He got into real estate and became rich. He even was a founder of a bank. His lovely wife Virginia was also in AA and they helped literally 100s of new people.

To make a long story short, I got drunk, and both my sponsor and Tom stayed sober. The next I heard of Tom was his wife had developed a brain tumor. She died a terrible death. He was unable to cope with her death. In 1983 he walked out of his home and stuck a .38 Ruger in his mouth and pulled the trigger.

To say the least AA in the area was shaken to its core, but AA survived. They even named a room after Tom where AA meets.

The gist of what I experienced: I finally got sober over a decade ago and married a wonderful woman. Both our first marriage. We had no children by choice and we had a great sober life. Sober wedding and sober life. In April 1996 my wife developed a tumor on her brain stem. There was nothing Mayo clinic etc. could do. She died in December '96. Seeing that I do not believe in a higher power etc. I could not end up hating god. I went through a lot of emotions that come when your mate and best friend dies. I did not drink.

Here are two non-believers: my sponsor who died sober after 30+ years and me (up to now) who did not throw in the towel. Tom didn't drink, but committed suicide either by choice or by circumstances beyond his control. Where was his god in his true time of need?

When it comes to doing the 12 steps in order or whatever AA preaches, I sure don't fit the mold. When people in AA learn my experience in life, there isn't anything they can say. Basically they leave me alone. Well this thread is a long one for me. Yours in not drinking,

John

6/14/98

The Most Positive Action I Have Ever Taken

By Lorne L.

[Lynn posted that she was one day sober.]

Hey, Greetings Lynn and welcome aboard the good ship RECOVERY!!

One day -- that's just great. You know, Lynn, we all have just one day -- today. The past is history and the future isn't here so now is what we have. It takes great courage to make the decision to quit drinking. You have made the choice. That's the big one and you've done it. The rest will fall into place with honesty and determination.

Really, though, you just have to do it for now. The decision I made to quit drinking has been the life-saving, most positive action I have ever taken. When I quit, the game was over for me. The doctor told me that continued drinking would see me dead in less than 2 years. My mind was a mess, my marriage was nearly done and my employer was really upset with me. You see, I was a deputy sheriff and a drunk in that business is bad, bad news. Near the end I remember sitting in a sheriff's vehicle I had driven to some isolated alley and seriously contemplating using the service revolver -- well that's kind of hard to think about.

But I didn't and today I am sober and I tell you it's the greatest feeling to have. My employer helped me and as I got sober my mental and physical health improved each day. My marriage stayed and we just had our 27th anniversary. Yes, Lynn, there's lots of feelings and emotions but, as a great American statesman once said, "there is nothing to fear but fear itself."

As I look back now, when I was in my early days of sobriety, what I was afraid of was being afraid. The emotions and feelings I learned to understand by sharing with others just like me. Sobriety is a great thing, Lynn, you learn to live free from booze and drugs. You learn to live with dignity as a person worthy of the best you can do.

I have said to a few people on this list that no one has any more right to recovery than anyone else. We are all people wanting the same thing - a decent and happy life. It does happen -- it does!! I have seen it happen in many lives. Just stick around and use this list. I just recently discovered it and think it is the best thing in recovery I have seen for a long time.

I could only tell you my story, Lynn, I hope, in some small way it helped. I have been sober now since 1986. Take care, Lynn, tomorrow is another '1 day'. Use this list and feel free to contact me anytime.

A friend in sobriety,
Lorne

6/19/98

Why I Drank Like I Did

by Tom S.

I spent a lot of time, most of it drinking, trying to "figure out" why I drank like I did. I assumed, owing to circumstances in my family, that I was mentally ill and that my drinking was a means of "self-medicating." I assumed that the pressures of my job and family caused me to drink to blot out or erase those situations with which I had to deal. I assumed that I drank like I did because I liked to, and, that it was normal and appropriate behavior, both personally and culturally.

Well, at least from my present perspective, all of my assumptions were wrong. I found that I drank like I did because ... I drank like I did. I drank like I did as a result of my biology, my metabolism. Certainly, many things internal and external affected my drinking, but the "reason" for my drinking like I did was, simply, that I could. I was unable to drink in any other fashion.

With that understood, I was then able to get about the business of doing something about the "rest of my life." To that end, I got some counseling, a different job, involvement with other sober people, and began to assemble the myriad other bits and pieces that have gone together to make the fabric of a new, sober, life.

I hope I haven't beaten this one to death, I just want to make the point that drinking, as we do, is the product of our biology and not a result of bad choices, character defects, or any of a thousand other spurious causal factors.

Spend time on those things that will improve your sober life and leave behind the quest for "why," it is a "how" question, anyway.

June 29, 1998

Poem

By Jette P.

Dried out skin and wrinkles galore
Baggy eyes, fatigue and more
Bloated belly and bulging hips
Bleeding gums and cracking lips
Troubled sleep and cramping toes
Blackouts, despair and many more woes
Why on earth continue drinking
knowing how deep and fast I'm sinking.

[Submitted by a Bradenton FL SOS member who is not on the net but wanted to share it; posted by Mark P.]

16 Jun 1998

A Chance to Start Over

By Shirlee B.

[Don wrote: Plus, I tend to get angry more than I liked and that is a drag and so I did not want to practice getting mad.]

Don,

I stumbled across this myself just recently only it has more to do with why I am "sad" rather than "mad." Why keep dredging up this old anger stuff and negativity, then write it down and share it with more people, and reinforce it. Lucky you were thrown out. :)

If I want to learn to be a more positive person I have to "act as if I am a positive person"... So I decided a few days ago to just try to keep my writing and thoughts centered on the "glad" occasions and practice writing out positive statements about my life and myself. And it is amazing what a battle it is to do this. I have to chuck out almost all the past 52 years of seeing everything as what I "can't" do, what I am "not allowed to do," start over, and now proceed with what I "can" do.

Being sober has given me a chance to start my life over; not to redo sober what I did while drinking, but to have a whole new way of doing everything. Now before I censor what I just wrote and start hearing in my head about punctuation not being right, and what are "they" going to think, it's not good enough, etc, etc., yada, yada, yada ... I will send this off.

Shirlee

5 June 1998

At First You Fall Down a Lot

By Craig M.

[Jan wrote: I sure am having trouble staying sober....]

Jan -

You don't really sound like you enjoy drinking at all anymore. I remember the last months of my drinking — hating every drop of vodka I poured down my throat, yet sneaking out and buying another "last" bottle ... every single day.

Once I had decided that I had a problem with alcohol, I was never able to unambiguously enjoy it again — and I suspect that is true for a lot of people. That alone will not keep you from drinking, just from enjoying it.

For me a key realization was: "From now on, you will never be able to drink without feeling a little bad. There's nothing you can ever do to change that, it's like trying to run around the house 50 times without thinking of elephants — once you realize that alcohol is killing you, you can't even try to suppress the thought without thinking it."

The key thing that got me sober was an accident, but something I could have arranged if I had looked into myself a little deeper. I had all the pieces to the puzzle. Anyway, I have a deep aversion to authority, always have and always will. So this AA-nut-chemical-counselor-who-I-have-to-see-because-that's-what-my-insurance-sends-me-to says "You're too stubborn, too much denial. You're not at a bottom, and I don't think you're ready to quit yet."

Of course the only reaction available in my emotional palette is: "Fuck you. I can too. I'll show you, bitch." And I haven't had a drink since.

So what is it that makes you tick? When you're too tired to care and can't even imagine getting up off the couch, what can shoot your blood pressure up 50 points and get you moving? How can you use your strengths (and turn what you might think are your weaknesses into strengths) to beat the bottle?

Right now, I hope you can dump the booze that you have and not buy more. You slipped up last night, that's pretty common.

Stopping drinking is like learning to ride a bicycle. At

first you fall down a lot. You might get mad at the bike, at your parents who bought you that dumb bike that doesn't work right, or even at people who aren't having as hard a time learning to balance. But if you keep trying, you eventually "get it" — the falls cease or become very rare, isolated experiences which certainly don't mean "you can't do it." It becomes effortless most of the time, something you don't even have to think about.

Keep trying and take care of yourself,
Craig

20 Jul 1998

Breaking a Lifelong Pattern

by Jane D.

[Jan had posted: Sorry couldn't take it any longer. Had to drink, poor judgment but felt good (actually bad). How can I stop, I can't talk to you guys immediately and I was waiting for some inspirational mail and that didn't come.]

Wow! I've been feeling just like that for the last week. Couldn't take it any longer. Major confrontations with mistakes I've made in the past. And even some I'm just about sure I'll make in the future. Felt it would be a relief to drink (even though I knew it would also make me feel bad). I couldn't wait for inspirational email either -- had no access. I felt hurt, and lonely and abused. I felt there was no way out of old patterns -- they hurt just a bit too badly.

Made a conscious effort to remember the sobriety priority. Don't drink, no matter what. Sounded so simplistic, so trivial, so remote -- how does this alleviate or even explain the pain? How does it heal gnawing guilt? How is this going to make me a whole person? What's the point?

Slapped myself in the head. I know I am better sober than drunk. Ok, that's a start.

When I think about all the stupid risks I've made in my life, the "risk" of trying to live it sober seems so small. Drunk is life-threatening. Sober opens possibilities.

At my family's house, my sister asked me what I wanted to drink with dinner. I said, water. When she put a glass of wine (my drug of choice, more, the one-time love of my life) by my place setting, I asked her for WATER. When my mother asked me why I wasn't drinking the wine, I, for the first time to my family, said, I am an alcoholic and I can't drink. She said abruptly and unkindly, "you're NOT an alcoholic, one glass won't hurt you." The half-hour conversation that followed was one of the longest of my life. But, long enough for me to finally perceive that they were more uncomfortable with it than I (long discussion about alcoholism in my family).

And, it was liberating cause I saw myself breaking a lifelong pattern. Part of it was, for me, trying to live in the moment (not worrying about coulda, shoulda, woulda), and part of it was not to betray the newly forming trust my children are building in me.

Think I must have read “Drinking At” a dozen times a day. Stupid me finally figured out, after all that reading, that I really didn't WANT to drink, I just wanted all of them to stop being at me. Drinking doesn't stop it. So, I didn't drink.

I'm learning, (all the time lately, thank the goddess!!) that I don't have to react. And the world isn't all about me, but it's not about them either.

Jane.

17 Jul 1998

Big Stuff Going On

By Laura L.

Dear Group:

I don't know what I might accomplish by doing this, maybe I will get lucky and help myself, as well as someone else.

As some of the folks who have been on here know, I have been going through a very difficult time. The die has been cast, and I will be getting a divorce from my husband, F., when the law allows it. In NC, that means one year of separation. I am as OK with the breakup of my marriage as I suppose anyone can be.

In the meantime, having moved out on my own, I have been sampling the many delights that an Army base full of horny young GIs has to offer. Of all things, I actually developed a crush on a fellow, who has summarily dumped me; I found this out today. He is "so sorry" and "really likes me" and all that other bullshit that people say to ease their own consciences.

In the meantime, I have developed yet another lump in my breast (third one in 18 months) but the doc is hanging back on doing any more "invasive" stuff. Probably just a fibroid anyway.

Add to this the pressure of a job that has just about put me over the edge. As someone who is used to working in the private sector, my experience with local government can only be likened to a pain tolerance test. In the Army, this is called "failure to adapt."

I have failed to adapt, and that may be the only source of pride that I currently have. I have cried, off and on since 10AM today; I actually had to leave my office because of uncontrollable crying. A wonderful thing for all the new employees there for orientation to see! In fact, I have started crying again just thinking about all this shit. How do small children do this without going insane?

At any rate, with the recent discussion on suicide, I wanted to add my own two cents worth. Although the idea is tempting, I am simply too pissed off to let anybody off the hook.

As far as drinking goes, the facts are as such: I am at the lowest point that I have been since I stopped drinking. I really am. I know it, and I am scared. But the thing that I am scared of is not so much taking a drink or using, it is that I feel that it may be necessary, if this gets worse, to go into some kind of in-patient psychiatric facility. But I will do that, and without hesitation, if I feel my sobriety is threatened.

My psychiatrist is aware of all this, and has been really good about not suggesting fast-acting sedatives or anything that might "wake up" my lizard brain.

The bottom line is this: my life sucks and is presently in a complete f**king shambles. But I am not going to drink "at" it, over it, or try to drink my way "around" it. This is big stuff going on, and I am going to need to have my wits about me to get through all this. I am angry, frightened, sad, horny, pissed off and I can't sleep worth a "dayum." Hell, at least I'm not bored! And feeling all this stuff just absolutely beats the hell out of feeling ... nothing ... numb ... drunk.

Fondest regards to all.

Laura

8 Jul 1998

Sober Is Better

By Paula B.

Dear Jan,

I've had a delightful 4th, followed by a decadent night eating fresh raspberries, blueberries & watermelon while watching pure trash on TV. It don't get no better than this. I left my email notification program on, heard the beep & wandered out to find your message.

I read your earlier message about being too-what-have-you to understand why you couldn't stop, and I have a suggestion for you. Instead of thinking about all the things that you (undoubtedly) are, and why can't you stop, try thinking that you're gonna stay sober, no matter what, & see what happens.

I have friends on this list who are sober through family illnesses, family deaths, their own serious illnesses (I'm one), their joys in motherhood, their career successes & failures, being victimized by crime and accident and adversity, and all of us who are making it are doing it because, at times, we are willing to settle for an uncomfortable sobriety. For us, and perhaps for you, uncomfortable sobriety beats 'comfortable' drunk all to hell.

In my current sober life, I'm an unemployed 44 year old woman, living with 8 ferrets of my own, plus 4 evacuated ferrets from the Florida fires, one dog and one cat. Only one of my animals was store bought, all the rest are rescues or fosters. My rent is paid for several months, and I'm taking some time off to write my history because I want it recorded. I'm awaiting results of more testing to see if my cancer has recurred, and have stopped smoking to help make those tests negative. A lot of this stuff is uncomfortable (do you have any idea how much poop twelve ferrets can create???), but sober is still better.

This is MY life, and I'm living it free from chemical intervention or interpretation, and sober is better than drunk. Something happened with me to change my value system from wanting to be drunk to wanting sobriety. I think it had to do with how I looked drunk, with the loneliness of drinking at the end of it, with my contempt for myself and the lies

I had to tell to keep it going … my drinking hurt more than sobriety ever could.

Maybe you can sidestep all the why can't I stuff, commit yourself to sober, no matter what & see what happens. I hope so. While I wait to find out, I'm gonna let Cady the Dawg out, eat a bowl of Cranberry Almond Crunch with milk and Equal, pet Kelsey the cat, check on the ferrets, and set the sleep timer on cable for zoning….

Join us, Jan. Sober is better.

Best Independent hugs,

Paula

05 Jul 1998

Woke Up Thankful

By Colleen C.

Hi gang: Well my cousin who lives here in Nashville asked me to go the stock car races last night so she could peruse the sea of blue collar boys and hopefully snake charm one. I obliged wondering if I would drink. Dumb maybe but .... She was a little stunned when I said I didn't want a beer, and boy, beer was aplenty, vendors everywhere and everywhere someone with a beer in hand. Nashville is a chain smokin' drinkin' town. She remembers what a fun drunk I was and was clearly disappointed when I didn't join her. The races in fact were thrilling for about two hours then I got tired of the noise. If I had been drinking, this natural curve from enjoyment to wanting it to be over would have been replaced with wanting it to go and on so I could drink, not knowing when to leave the damn fair. Woke up thankful I hadn't caved in. Bless me.

12 Jul 1998

I Don't Drink Because ...

By Jim M.

Everyone,

I want to thank the whole list for congratulating me on my anniversary! Thank you Laura, Carol, Marianne, Bernie, Colleen, Dana, Mark, Shirley, Jim, Rex, Michael, Peggy, Michael H., Larry, Randy, Marjorie, Barbara, Robert, Phil, Don, Scott and Teri, Bonnie, and Marty for thinking of me today :o) And to anyone I didn't list: Thank you too! :o)

I spent the day getting the truck fixed, eating lunch at a Mexican restaurant in a small strip mall, sleeping about 5 hours (I work nights) and generally doing everyday stuff. My wife brought me a peanut butter cup with a single candle on it! LOL! :o)

Some have asked me to say how I did it. Well, I think the first and foremost thing that comes to mind is to NOT DRINK. Easier said than done, I know. I would never tell anyone that it was easy. But it wasn't so difficult, for me, either. I've told many people from the beginning that I wasn't going to drink again. I meant it. But perhaps the single most "eye opening" factor was the KNOWLEDGE of what alcoholism is and is not. I learned all I could about what happened to me physically and mentally. I learned that this is basically a difference in body makeup and that I am different than 90% of normal drinkers, who can take it or leave it. There's more to it than that but, in short, I don't drink because I KNOW now that if I drink I will die, or worse.

Of course, my family support and support from friends like you all helps a lot!

Thank you again, everyone, for being here. On to the next year! :o)

13 Jul 1998

The "Just-One" Genie

By Diane J.

Pauli, you wrote well about the "Just-One" Genie:

> *<snip>Rest of the family knows I'm in a program and either not drinking or only "one." Yeah, it's terrible and causes me enormous problems. But a couple of "just ones" in a week is so much better than 18 months ago; I'm putting up with it for now. This is not my goal, however. I have really proven to myself that having just one sets me up to do it again.*

I winced when I read this, a little, because I got a fairly lethal visit from the "Just-One" Genie (I LOVE the name) five and a half years ago after I got out of "treatment." I hated the place, hated AA, was miserable and depressed, but had sort of decided to stay sober... (OK, NOT a good frame of mind....laugh). I even found one of the very early (first incarnation) Rational Recovery groups. Got home for Christmas, two months sober -- and COULDN'T WOULDN'T deal with all of the subtle pressure to "drink like a normal person" and PROVE I wasn't "one of those people in there."

So I decided I'd just drink a little over Christmas and get sober again in January. Did it, too. There, proved THAT, didn't I? Now, EASTER, on the other hand ... it took me a little LONGER to get sober again, but I did it. And then, since I'd proved to myself I COULD drink under "special circumstances" and get sober again ... well, why couldn't I just drink at parties? After all, that would only be once or twice a month ... well, there, you see, I can do THAT ... so why couldn't I maybe have a drink with dinner on Friday nights? Just one, mind you, and just on Friday ... which would be only one drink a week, except for weeks with parties or visits or holidays in them, but hey, how many of those ARE there?

And, well, okay, if you're going to have a drink with dinner on Friday you probably ought to buy a bottle of vodka, but it's not like you're going to DRINK any just because it's in the cupboard, after all, are you? I mean, it's not like bottles jump out and MAKE you drink them.... (Anybody see a pattern emerging here yet? -- laugh.)

I don't think, after I was off and running, that I was two days in a row sober for the next four years. All I can tell you is it was a hell of a setup for me, that couple of "just ones" in a week.

It sounds to me like you've seen a danger in it for yourself and are working yourself away from it. Good for you. I know how hard that is, when all the pressure is to smooth the issue over and having "Just One" WILL do it. It really will, too. But you can never tell when it's a present from the "Just-One" Genie, I don't think.

You write:

> *So---I tell you because I don't think I can handle the shame with my counselors tomorrow. I think this trip home is the last experience with the "just one" genie. I think, I hope and I intend to make it happen; but I will not beat myself up if I ever slip.*

Pauli, don't shame yourself. And your counselors should certainly know better than to think that shaming someone is either generous or productive. You've learned a lot from this trip; your posts show that. And by talking to us about it, you'll get many ideas for how to handle the situation more to your liking next time. There should be no question of shame. Be proud of yourself for recognizing the subtle traps in the situation and for thinking about how to make that the "Just-One" Genie's last appearance.

Take care,
Diane J.

Aug. 1998

Why I Didn't Keep Coming Back

By Trudy S.

Sometimes I drive by the building where a lot of our local AA meetings are held, and when the parking lot is full, I wonder if there"s anybody else like me in there. Once I saw a woman standing alone by her car, fumbling for something in her purse, in obvious distress. I could recall myself in the same place years ago, knowing I would never, ever go back in there again.

You see, there is AA, and there is AA. Of course, things may have changed in the eleven years since I've attended a meeting, but in those days groups differed from state to state. I'd started out in Michigan, with a "home group" that emphasized the fellowship and sharing aspects of the Program, and soft-pedaled the 12 Steps. At a meeting, people sat at tables of six or eight people, giving everyone the chance to talk or not, as they chose. There was a "topic of the day," but that was only a suggestion for those who didn't have something in mind. I wasn't entirely comfortable with the concept of "powerlessness." There were many times I felt frustrated by the idea of standing around talking about how I wasn't drinking for the rest of my life, but the people were kind and caring, and this was the first group of people I'd ever encountered that accepted me the way I am. I never felt like "the odd one out" at those meetings, nobody ever pointed out the fact that I'm just not like other people. (I read too much and too fast; I bake from scratch and around that time I liked to take the neighborhood kids down to the park to hug trees.)

Once in a while my sponsor and I would take in a different meeting, to broaden our horizons. I wondered what "good, quality AA" was. I'd hear the term a lot, and it didn't quite make sense to me. Going to different meetings -- and there were dozens, if not hundreds in the Detroit area -- was my way of finding that out. We'd encounter serious, by-the-Book AA people, and they never hesitated to point out the error of our ways. We'd shrug it off, secure in the knowledge we always had our own, comfortable meeting to go to four times a week. I went on like this for almost two years.

I lived with my husband and our little boy in what is now

called "the Inner city" of Detroit, and our neighborhood was changing. We had lived there for eight years, since our son was born, and we had seen the neighbors go from young families like us, who owned their own homes, to single mothers who rented. Many of our neighbors were on welfare now, and Sean was one of only five white kids at his elementary school. We began to feel the tension of racism to the point where we began to feel it was no longer a safe place for us to live. It was time to go.

Even though we knew money would be tight, our major concern was to have our son grow up in a place where he could go to a decent school and maybe get involved in Boy Scouts. We chose Arizona mainly because my parents were already here, and the winters were mild. I looked forward to meeting new people through AA. At my first meeting with the Michigan group, I kept thinking of my little boy's first time at a park. He leapt out of the stroller, shouting, "Friends!" and ran across the grass as fast as he could. That's how that meeting was for me. I couldn't know how different the AZ group was going to be.

I got a list of meetings, and in this small town, it was only a single sheet, triple-spaced. I expected that. So, the next morning, I found the meeting for that day, and off I went. Unfamiliar with the streets, I had a little trouble locating the address, which turned out to be a house in a residential area, right off the main street of town. My intention was to show up early, but I was actually a minute or two late. There was a man standing by the front door, and as I went up the steps, he said, "You're late." "Yeah, I had a little trouble finding it. I'm new," I said. "You're new? Who sent you?" As if there was some kind of password, and I couldn't go in unless I knew it. "Uh, nobody sent me -- I just moved here from Michigan." Was this the right place? "This is the AA meting, isn't it?" He stared at me for a minute before he opened the door. "Yeah, this is it. Be on time next time." When I went inside, the place was packed. The place had been a house at one time, but most of the interior walls had been removed, leaving one big room. Only the kitchen was separate. There were no tables, and everybody was seated on a collection of donated living room furniture. A footstool was in a corner, the only place I could see to sit, and I grabbed it.

The meeting had already started, apparently, but I couldn't see anything going on at the front of the room. I could hear people talking, but not make out the words. Well, maybe I'd get there earlier next time. After a long time, everybody stood up. I still couldn't hear anything, but people started heading for the door, and within minutes I was alone. I hadn't spoken to anybody but the bouncer at the door. I could hear voices coming from out back somewhere, but I didn't want to run into the bouncer again. All I could do was shrug and go home. Next time I would get there early.

The next day I was there a full half-hour early. Nobody was around, and I went back to kitchen, where I found an older lady filling a coffee urn with water. I offered to help, and she looked at me like I'd lost my mind. "Oh, no, you'd just get in the way," she said. I didn't know what to say to that. The meetings in MI were always looking for volunteers for something or another.

Not wanting to invade anyone's territory, I went out and sat in the big room alone. Occasionally somebody would come in and inform me that I was early, and then head for the kitchen. Nobody stopped to talk. At least I found out how the meetings went. The chairperson for the day chose the subject, and then she would choose people to speak on that subject. It didn't seem that anyone was bold enough to speak on something else. Then when time was up, everybody left.

I went to this meeting several times, and it was always the same thing. There was a small group of people that clustered in the kitchen before the meeting, and the same group was chosen to speak. I didn't see anybody exchange phone numbers; in fact the rest of the people attending hardly spoke to one another at all.

I tried another, smaller meeting earlier in the day, and it was the same story here. Don't show up early, don't hang around after. I did try to get phone numbers, but I was either told, "I don't give out my number," or the person didn't have a phone. (It's true there are a lot of people that don't have phones here.) Because of the size of the meeting, I was chosen to speak on occasion, and I went there regularly for awhile.

I also tried a women's meeting where the people were at least polite, if distant. That was the oddest thing; I expected a women's group to be more open, more inclined to welcome newcomers, but there wasn't much difference. I went to every meeting on my sheet, except for the one held in a restaurant. I couldn't afford to pay for dinner out. So, for a few months I went to the women's group, and the small meeting, even though it had become a chore. I just couldn't seem to connect with anyone. There didn't seem to be any social element here for those who weren't part of the inner circle that ran everything. After one lady turned me down with a flat "no," I didn't bother asking anyone else to be my sponsor, and I knew there was no point in asking for phone numbers.

Then, two things happened that were the end of AA for me. First, I had a slip. I made the mistake of talking about it in a meeting. (This was the only variation in the routine I ever saw. Sometimes a guy would talk about a slip, and that was OK.) I won't bore you with the details, but after I spoke, the rest of the meeting I was chewed out for "not working my Program." That was the reason I had a slip, and it was all my fault. I had to accept the second step, or I was going to die. That was it. These people that had never spoken to me for longer than thirty seconds suddenly knew everything about me and what I should do to fix it. I was dumfounded, too upset to even try defending myself. As the meeting broke up, I went out to the kitchen to put my coffee cup in the trash, and the good ole boys at the kitchen table actually laughed and pointed!

It took me a week to get up the nerve to go to another meeting. Thinking the women's group was the better choice (most of them hadn't been there when I put my foot in it!), I showed up but not expecting to say anything. Whatever the subject was, I would pass. A woman in her late 20s showed up a minute or two late and sat next to me. I said hello to her, even though the meeting had started, despite the dirty look from the chair. Her name was Carla. When it came time for me to talk, I passed, and it was Carla's turn. She was court-ordered, terrified, and she didn't know where her kids were. That was all she was able to say before she broke down. I put my arm around her, and found her a tissue in my purse. After a few moments of stunned silence, the next woman in line spoke, and the meeting went on. I went in the kitchen and got Carla a cup of coffee, and some more tissues. I offered her a ride home, and my phone number. By then, the meeting was over. Carla had somebody coming for her, so she didn't need a ride.

I was the last to leave, and the chairperson came over and explained to me "that isn't how we handle court-ordereds," and I should've let "somebody with some quality sobriety behind them" handle the situation. I had no idea how she would know what the quality of my sobriety was, since she had made no attempt whatsoever to get to know me. Apparently she presumed that since I was new to her group, I was also new to sobriety.

In hindsight, I wish I'd had the strength to explain my personal quality of two plus years of sobriety to her in words of one syllable, but that was more than I could do then. All I could do was walk out, too angry and hurt to talk back. I had not "worked my Program," I had broken the rules, I was worthless and it was all my fault. There was no other choice. Work the Program or die. Since their damn Program didn't look like it was going to work for me, I guessed I would probably die.

I carried this around with me for years. I had periods of months of sobriety, interspersed with periods of drinking. Occasionally I'd get out the books, looking for some kind of motivation or reassurance, but the answer was always the same. I had failed the Program.

In 1990, my husband entered a 5-day detox program, and started going to AA meetings almost every day. He already knew some of the members through his work, and had no problem settling in. This might have encouraged me to try it again, but instead it only reinforced the idea that something was wrong with me.

One day I was at my desk where I worked for a private charity, when a psychologist and a social worker visited my boss for some reason. They were talking about a family where two alcoholics had small children and were court-ordered to attend AA meetings. The social worker remarked that the woman was “not very strong, I hope she can handle it." The psychologist answered, "AA here is just terrible, some people it does more harm than good."

They went on to talk about this particular case, but what they had said about AA really struck home. I began to wonder if maybe there was some hope for my problem after all. If AA wasn't effective sometimes and a psychologist admitted it, maybe there was something else. But what?

There was a whole shelf in our local library devoted to addiction and recovery, but it was all AA material. In those days there was a lot happening with my family, including the death of my mother. Sometimes it seemed that the trouble would never end. I began to question authority, my religion, everything.

When I first went on-line in early ‘96, the Internet fascinated me. I discovered the religious group I belonged to was considered a cult by some. I read with great interest all the material I could find. It was no surprise when references to AA started popping up. I began to realize that by belonging to AA, the only thing that is happening for me is swapping one addiction for another, albeit more socially acceptable one.

The founders of the organization were not looking to the future, and probably never expected it to last over 60 years. They created AA in line with rigid, Protestant Christian ideals, and at the time the Program made good sense for most people. In the 30s and 40s, however, life was different than it is now. Authority was respected and rarely questioned, and the term, "God-fearing Christian" was synonymous with, "good upstanding person." Today a good, upstanding person may be a Hindu, agnostic, or even atheist. High moral and ethical standards are not exclusively Christian values.

As the scientific research into addiction progressed, a mistaken parallel was drawn relating AA as a recovery program with the disease of alcoholism itself. The well-known Jellinek chart shows the progression of the disease, with the last stage being recovery or death. Since AA was the only recovery program at the time, the members of AA saw recovery as being synonymous with AA. So, somehow the accepted logic became "AA or death."

The concept of alcoholism as a character flaw was never quite eliminated as it should have been, either, because one of the basic concepts of Christianity is that human beings are by nature, flawed. There's a funny thing about Christians -- they simply refuse to acknowledge the existence of any other religion. AA appears to be the same. With more and more people joining AA over the decades and becoming indoctrinated into the philosophy, the idea of some other treatment mode being effective was neglected. Science and society progressed, while AA remained unchanged.

AA itself is unlikely to change; in fact there is no reason why it should, since it does work for those who are willing to accept AA's dogma. What should change is the availability of alternative treatment methods. Programs such as SOS and Women for Sobriety do exist and have proven to be effective, but are available only on a limited basis. There is no "magic pill" right now, but research continues and there may be a medical therapy someday.

The general public needs to be made aware that a person who resists AA is not necessarily resisting sobriety. There is plenty of room for many groups and alternative therapies, as there are for other diseases such as arthritis and cancer. Above all, what the alcoholic needs is hope; hope for something else, something more that could lead to the beginnings of a normal life.

August 1998

At War Within Myself

By Marty N.

When I drank, I was a man at war within myself. This war had many fronts. There was the intellectual war, between the 'me' that saw my life falling apart, and the other 'me' that constructed a reason to drink from every event. There was the war of feelings: the revulsion at my enslavement by the bottle, the self-hatred, the feeling of powerlessness and panic, v. the sticky-sweet surrender to inebriation, the irresistible embrace of oblivion. At the deepest level it was the war of life v. death within me, and death, liquid death, was winning.

An unexpected passing word from a dearly loved one -- "Dad, you are a drunkard, isn't that right?" -- exploded over the battlefield like a brilliant flare one afternoon. Called my HMO, signed up for the "Alcohol and Drug Abuse Program," had my last drink (Oct. 1, 1992), started program sessions, started attending outside support group meetings. Was fortunate to find SOS from day one. I've done my entire sobriety in SOS. No slips, no relapses, so far. I am asked here to explain "how it works." I have no idea. All I can tell you is how it works for me.

The really important assumptions are the unspoken ones. From day one, there was this basic assumption in the air at those SOS meetings that you -- we, I -- could stay sober if we worked at it. That it was possible. That, despite all the evidence to the contrary, there was the power within each of us to stop killing ourselves and start living. The proof was, simply, that we were doing it. People didn't dwell at length on their drinking histories -- the talk is more oriented to what's going on this week, today, right now -- but it took little time for me to see that I was among peers. Every stupid thing I had done under the influence met with resonant, laughing echoes. Week after week they came back with stories of victories in skirmishes with situations and people that once "drove them to drink." It was possible for someone like me to live a normal life and not drink! It was possible to win, not just lose! That was a big revelation to me at the time.

Nobody in my years in SOS has ever suggested that there

was a Program I had to or ought to follow to stay sober, other than "don't drink." No group ever suggested to me that I needed to surrender my judgment to its collective wisdom -- I would have walked out instantly. A few boring people did have the habit of giving unsolicited advice, telling other people how they should stay sober, but everyone ignored them. It has always been the assumption that no matter how long I had been drinking and no matter how deep I had sunk, I was competent to be, in Dr. Judith Herman's felicitous phrase, "the author and arbiter of my own recovery."

Since I was a daily drinker, I built my recovery practice around the "Daily Do." Before he left AA, SOS founder Jim Christopher surveyed some 200 people with long-term sobriety and asked them what it was that had kept them that way. "We reaffirm our sobriety every day." Exactly what you do, what form you give that affirmation, doesn't much matter. Sometimes I said phrases, sometimes I took vitamins, sometimes I set an alarm, nowadays I work email, every day, with sobriety in mind.

The SOS philosophy, if there is such a thing, is extremely simple. Two words express it: Sobriety Priority. I take that to mean that staying sober is the most important thing I need to keep in mind when I come to any fork in the road. Sobriety is the foundation of everything else. Keep sobriety, I'm OK no matter what; lose sobriety, I lose everything else.

Oh, yes, the God thing. Outside people always ask about it. Somehow it never comes up in our meetings, or very rarely. We start, as I said, from the assumption that even the baddest of the bad has some good within them. In our fellowship we look for that good, we praise and encourage the heck out of it, we give it all kinds of mental, emotional and social support. We often end our meetings with a round of applause to ourselves for staying sober. And so it seems only natural to us that the "me" within each of us that wants to be sober does gradually get stronger and more confident, and takes charge of the person. Through our self-help mutual support process we help tip the war within each of us in favor of the sober forces. At least that was my experience. And I guess we're just so busy giving each other support for staying sober that we never get to the God thing. Going there seems like a detour. That's why we call ourselves "secular."

Many SOS members also attend AA or other 12-Step groups. We have no problem with that, as we are on the same journey, although by a different road. People tell me they like the atmosphere in our meetings because there's no cigarette smoke, no coffee, no cookies, and no preaching. They don't have to talk in formulas and slogans and be spiritually correct but can just drain their brain. They like having some time set aside for crosstalk. They like the mutual support and the sharing of experiences that they get both places. They wish we were bigger and had more meetings already. We're working on it.

8/98

Applause for the Struggling

By Gregg F.

Hi all, I just ran a 5K race this morning. The same race I wanted to run for the past two years. The same race I passed in my car last Labor Day, racing to the bar to get there as soon as it opened. A knot in my gut made worse by viewing the happy faces of the runners.

Something can be learned by me from the runners. It seems the people that struggled the most got the most support, cheers and applause. No one was judged because they didn't train harder, thus improving their performance. No, everyone was cheered on just the same for being in the race — actually a social run for most.

I think staying sober might be like running. Some of us alcoholically challenged may have an actual talent for staying sober, while for others it is a lot more difficult. I think that from now on I should applaud those even more that are having a difficult time, for there is a lot to say for someone just for being in the race. The motive for being there or the amount of training doesn't matter, but what matters is that they are with me in the same endeavor.

Those of us that have been doing really well for a long period of time stumble and get back up and go again should really be cheered for it is a challenge to begin again from this new perspective.

Marianne, I raise my diet soda to you this morn and say three cheers to ya. Three cheers to all of us.

Gregg F.

9/7/98

You Are Not a Failure

By De W.

Personal experience.... Sober 10 years, thought it would be absolutely no problem. Put myself in a very challenging situation, lapsed for 2 years while in that situation. Got my self out (actually not by choice, but it worked out) and now have 2 years again. What didn't work for me was believing in the one-drink-leads-to-a-drunk. That is what I drank to. Ok. So you fell down.

Here is something I wrote, when I had 24 hours this last time. Maybe it will help someone else.

Because You have a Failure, You are not a Failure.

I choose. I choose what path to follow. I choose which way to go. I may not consciously choose to fail, but I can choose to go in another direction when the failure comes to light. This is what I have been learning.

I am not what I do. If I make a mistake, I am not a mistake. If I do bad things, I am not a bad person.

I am inherently good. Whether or not I do anything with my life, my life has meaning. If I have a failure, it does not mean I am a failure. If I slip it doesn't mean I am lost. Negative thinking is just that: Thinking. It is not "reality." If I put my negative thoughts into action, I have chosen to do so.

Whatever I do at any given moment is what I perceive to be the best action. Two seconds later it might seem like the worst possible thing I could have done. In the moment of the decision however, it may have seemed to be to my advantage. I can change the direction at any time. I can be honest about the action taken and move on to the next one.

That's important for me to admit and move on. Dwelling on it doesn't help.

I am scared to death to break my abstinence. I can hear myself dare me to do it. I can make the choice not to. If I do however break my abstinence, I am not a failure. I am acting on a compulsion. I choose whether to continue the behavior. Bad behavior does not make a bad person.

People, humanity, is (if not good) at least neutral. My reason for existence is to do what I can to make a difference. A lot of this is regurgitated from other readings and hearings.

I am not sure I am totally convinced, except when I remember "I love you." "I am not convinced I deserve it." "You don't have to deserve it. IT JUST IS." Then I know I am something special. Failures and all. I am living proof that if you have a failure, you are not a failure. I keep picking myself up and moving on.***

I read this everyday for quite awhile and since my recent difficulty with new days/new beginnings I have it out again. I thought it might help someone else.

(The conversation was one I had with that 'still quiet voice' inside myself about 4 years into my first phase of recovery/discovery. It had a major impact on me then, and still does today.)

De W. -- Life is what happens while you are making other plans.

9/10/98

What Makes Me Want To Stay Sober?

By Kathy B.

[Responding to Lynda's question why sobriety is better than drinking]

What makes me want to stay sober? It's a great question. First, I'd have to say I never want to fall down on the pavement at 2AM and not remember what happened. Or ... being followed by some stranger in the wee hours of the morning and not realize the danger. Or ... risking a marriage because my husband has had to drag my amnesiac drunk body into the house for the umpteenth time.

What does it take? I enjoy waking up without my hands shaking in the morning, feeling wired to the gills because I need my dose of downer.

I enjoy the freedom I have found without the constant self-hatred.

I love the pride on my son's face when he talks about his sober alcoholic mother.

I love being able to dedicate myself to my work for the time that I am there and to be able to give of myself because I have something left to give.

I love sleeping at night without waking at 3AM feeling all nervous inside because my central nervous system is on overdrive and wondering how I'm going to make it the next fifteen or so hours without the help of the bottle which has now become my best friend in my mind but my worst enemy in reality.

I love being able to make a promise and keep it. And I love being able to sit still and at the same time feel at peace.

I certainly could go on because there are so many other reasons. Perhaps it would be helpful for you to write down a list of reasons why you want to stay sober vs. reasons why you want to drink.

Despite all that, whatever you decide is more worthwhile, your drinking will get more and more out of control, you will do more things that you regret having done and in the end, if you are like so many of us, you will die of your disease in a state of impoverishment not just of money but of intimacy and dignity. Sobriety sounds pretty good, doesn't it?

Kathy in Nashville

14 Aug 1998

365 Attaboys

By Steve C.

Steve out of San Jose, the consummate lurker here. I just thought I'd send in a message to fish some attaboys. I attained one year of sobriety yesterday, 21 Sep 1998.

No blackouts for 365 consecutive days. I've been able to find my car every morning, parked right outside for 365 consecutive days. Not so much as a traffic ticket for 365 days. No meaningless apologies to the wife, kids, and bartender in the morning for 365 days. I have woken up warm and cozy in my own bed for 365 consecutive days. I haven't found dozens of ATM slips in my wallet that had seriously depleted my funds for 365 consecutive days. No urine or crap in my pants for 365 days. No broken noses, bloody clothes, or black eyes for 365 days. No jail cells for 365 days. No serious arguments with the wife, no storming out of the house, no threatening of break-ups in my marriage for 365 days. No two hour long lectures to crying and scared kids for 365 days. No downing of 5 or 6 aspirin in the morning for 365 days. My stomach has settled down for about I'd say only 200 or so days, it took a while. No blank spots in my mind for 365 days. No memories being told to me for 365 days. No holes punched in the wall, kicks in the doors, broken windows, or door jambs for 365 days. No fondling of a shotgun to my mouth for 365 days. No waking up and walking through a mine field of broken glass, tossed furniture, or drywall dust for 365 days. No wasted days to hangovers for 365 days. A whole year and none of this has occurred. Wow.

Please excuse me now as I climb up on a huge pink cloud I see coming my way.

21 Sept. 98

Different Strokes

By Bill McD.

I think that part of -- and a big part, at that -- of the reason I "failed" during my first few attempts at sobriety is that I was cavalier about it. And I sure as shit wasn't honest; at one point I remember actually planning a relapse while in treatment. Fought the good fight, as they say, after that, but the deed was basically done.

One of the reasons that I love this list more and more is that we *can* all have different ways of facing up to sobriety. In fact, those differences are the basis of why this works, as near as I can tell. It's a far cry from being told "the way."

I have recently met too many people who diligently follow "the program," but aren't really doing a damn thing. And then they can't figure out why they relapsed. After all, they went to all those meetings.... And then the character flaw thing crops up again, basically starting a vicious cycle -- more meetings will help get rid of the flaws, etc. If you don't think, don't *actually* participate, don't listen and at least try to learn, then what good is any course of recovery?

Oct. 9, 1998

Nothing Less Than the Best

By Shirley B.

<*I am beginning to question how much my determination not to interfere with the pleasure of people close to me is generosity and how much of it is fear that they won't want to play with me any more if it's even a little trouble (smile). -- D.*>

I know what you mean. But during the last few months I had this turn-around about that. And now I figure people are lucky if "I" sit there and tolerate their drinking and/or drunken behavior. Which I do less and less.

I'm on this bowling team now as a sub and after the game of course everyone wants to go to the sponsoring bar or restaurant and have eats and everyone else on the team drinks except me and my husband. Plus we don't eat all that fried sh*t anymore. We have not told them we are alcoholics, just that we don't drink anymore. Anyway, they are constantly making comments about what we drink and eat. Like being healthy is a disease or something. I guess they think we feel deprived.

I used to feel uncomfortable that I was making THEM uncomfortable because of my choices. Well, this is bullsh*t. I'm speaking up next time someone makes another comment on what I don't drink or eat. What I will say I don't know, but I'm sure sick of feeling like *I'm* the one doing something weird.

< *I don't expect the world to stop for me.*>

Why the hell not? Others think YOU should stop your world for them.

There are lots of drinking occasions I accommodate, but how sensible is it for me to spend lots of time around the stuff? Or around friends who feel horribly inconvenienced by waiting a few hours for a drink of it?

If you are just accommodating and not enjoying it, dump it. Now, you know, I had this problem too of letting go of old situations with drinking pals and how I thought I'd never find anything else to do in this town. I just stopped looking back. I stopped everything actually, and started to look at what "I" enjoyed doing and if I had to do it alone I did it.

I started talking to the ladies in the aerobics class more and now there are 3 of us who are good buddies at the class and we are gradually starting to go to other events together outside of the class. But this has taken over 6 months to develop so it isn't overnight. I even went up to the instructor the other day and asked her if she wanted to run in the race with me. The point being you have to be the one to reach out for the life you want. (Figuring out what you want is another thing entirely <g>)

For too long we have hidden ourselves behind, under, in, and around booze. Why stay with and around people who are still doing that if you don't have to. We are free!

How will these decisions shape and be shaped by length of sobriety for me?

Frankly, I think it has more to do with expecting and accepting nothing less than the best for yourself!!

Oct. 10 1998

I Recognize My Mind Games

By Steve C.

I was about 9 months sober, in June of 1998, when my Dad moved in with my family because of his Lou Gehrig's disease progression. He drinks nothing without alcohol in it, which means I keep it around the house now. He can't move his hands, can't walk, and is beginning to have trouble standing up and swallowing, but he can still suck liquor through a straw. I didn't choose to have a confrontation over it with him because it's the last thing he enjoys that he can still do. Plus, from my own experience, you can't force anyone into sobriety. Prior to this, I had a 1/4 bottle of gin in the freezer for about 3 weeks after I got sober. Eventually, I poured it down the drain because I found myself thinking about it quite a bit.

Anyway, when dad first got here, his thing was warm beer and brandy which wasn't too bad, since I hate warm beer, and I never cared too much for brandy unless it was in egg nog. But now, since he has trouble swallowing thin liquids, he's changed to rum and coke, screwdrivers, and greyhounds. All drinks I used to enjoy. I have full liters of brandy, vodka, and rum sitting on my kitchen counter right now. If he gets peppermint schnapps, or switches to gin and tonic, I might really be in trouble. I find myself thinking about just a small sip now and then when I'm carrying his drink over to him, but I know better than to follow through.

But what is scary, is how frightfully easy it could be, just one little mental slip, just one little irrational thought, just one little raise of my arm, and bingo, I'll probably wake up in the hospital or in jail. I find it interesting, since I really hadn't craved it too much over the last three months, but for some reason, its creeping back into my consciousness. I find it is getting really hard to mix his drinks, put a straw in it, and then carry it over to him without triggering the little mind game of "just a little sip," or "just a taste." Actually, I think maybe the smell of the stuff is what is triggering it. Maybe I should just get a nose plug.

So, what I have been doing is just forcing the smarter part of my conscious to take over, and trying to ignore what

Trimpey calls "the beast." I know that for me, alcohol is extremely dangerous, and when I'm around it, I'm on dangerous ground. I also think the craving must have something to do with the smell of the alcohol, which must trigger something in my body. I'm really beginning to believe that alcoholism is really a disease triggered by a physical craving which causes the so called "mental obsession" (AA stuff) because I don't know how else to explain it.

Anyway, my wife has been extremely worried about the situation for the last four months, and I have kept telling her "don't worry" nobody is going to pour it down my throat, but me. But, recently, with the different liquors being brought into the house, it has gotten to be a little bit more worrisome for me due to the mental games that are going on again. I let her know this, and she is going to mix his drinks a little more often for me until I get over this weirdness.

So I guess what I'm saying, is we all have to deal with alcohol in our lives at some point or another, but it's our minds that may betray us. For me, I think it would be better to just get rid of all the stuff in the house, but I can't or won't do that unless I put my dad in a home or something. Plus, I know that deep down, the stuff isn't going to magically come out of the bottle and land in my throat. I'm at least happy that I can recognize my mind games for what they are.

Oct. 10, 1998

Proud to Say It

By Marianne H.

There is absolutely no shame in being a sober alcoholic. On the contrary, it's something to be very, very proud of.

At first I, too, didn't want to tell anybody. Looking back, I think it was because I was afraid that if others knew that *I* knew I was alcoholic, I would be ashamed to have them see me drinking ever again, and I didn't want to give up that very tempting thought that if I just got myself under control, I might get to where I could have just one Brandy Manhattan on a special occasion.

Well, this list taught me the whys of what I already knew -- that for me, there was no such thing as one drink occasionally. And as I stayed sober longer after each relapse, I found myself feeling proud of my accomplishment. Because I knew just how hard it had been for me. Still is, for that matter.

Don't get me wrong. I don't go around volunteering to everybody and their Aunt Sadie that I'm a sober alcoholic. But when the situation (pre-op exam, or explaining my involvement in www.unhooked.com, for example) makes "I'm a sober alcoholic" appropriate, I'm damn fine proud to say it. And not one person has reacted badly, on the spot or later. Plus, I'm amazed at how many people have responded with "I'm one, too." Or "So is my daughter." "Boss." "Best friend." Etc.

Be proud of every sober day. There are an awful lot of alcoholics in this world who don't have the strength and determination (courage, too, I have come to think) that you've shown in getting these sober days strung together for yourself.

Oct. 21, 1998

Secret Code 505

By Nolita

I was beeped today in the middle of yet another stressful interview with a client. The page read "505," which in "SOS-speak" translates to "SOS." This is a trick we do in the Tampa Bay area to let each other know we are with them in spirit! I have an idea who it was from, but that is not the point. I received it in the spirit in which it was intended -- with a secret smile to myself! Thank you to whomever sent it!! Fellow SOSers--Try this on your friends!!

Oct. 21, 1998

Day One Again

By John E.

I have had so many "Day 1, Agains" over the past 15 years. The first Day 1 found me physically exhausted and weakened beyond reasonable imagination. The next to latest Day 1 found me emotionally and intellectually broken and scarred. The latest Day 1 found me coldly angry and determined to recover.

My Day 1s have been bizarre emotional experiences. Sometimes part of me would be afraid I was going to die and I would be found with my racing heart having ejected itself from my body and my skin having painfully crawled to another room. Another part of me was afraid I would never die and I would have to live my life feeling this way forever. I had literally and quite successfully created my own 24 hour Technicolor hell.

Exactly eight weeks ago I had another Day 1. The latest relapse was about 6 weeks in length after a 6 year abstinence. For good or for ill when I woke up the last still drunk morning I wasn't ashamed of myself. I just knew I had to stop drinking. I wasn't afraid of what the next few days would bring, I just had to stop drinking. I checked into a hospital and essentially said, "Keep me safe for a couple of days until I can begin to take care of myself again." There was no drama, no tears, no self flagellation. Just the simple unadorned knowledge that I had to stop drinking. Again.

After the 48 hour "rest" I came home and got prepared to fight this one more time. I wasn't sure how I was going to do it since AA was not particularly beneficial to me. Some people have allergies to penicillin, I have a mild allergic response to AA. But I made one important decision for me. I wasn't going to lie to myself anymore. I am an alcoholic who doesn't respond to AA so I have to find something else. Within 48 hours I had found the SOS web site and very soon started going to the one SOS meeting in Chicago. (Lucky for me someone decided to go to all the effort to start a meeting). After a fair amount of searching I hired a psychiatrist who specializes in alcoholism (recovering himself) and asked him to help me work through some issues that are bothersome. I met with my most important (financially) client and said, "Here's the situation. You decide what you need to do." There was a positive reaction to that. I began to put some of the disassembled pieces back in place.

I read this email list a couple of times a day. Each day someone writes something that contributes strength to my resolve not to drink that day. Each day I read the phrase "sobriety priority" and pay attention to it. Once a week I go to a meeting where a quiet calm supportive environment encourages me and reinforces the reality that this can work. Each day I am as truthful with myself as I know how to be.

For me it is a process. It's been going on for a long time, it has been exasperating and sometimes painful. But, it is the way I have had to do it. Of course life is already better. But then, of course I knew it would be. Just as I knew 14 weeks ago when I decided to drink, yet again, that my quality of life would almost immediately be diminished. But the nature of my alcoholism is that even though I knew negative things would happen, not drinking wasn't a priority. It wasn't important enough. It is today. And I'll just keep doing what I've been doing and I suspect that tomorrow will probably work out OK too.

It's a hell of a ride. Thanks for reminding me of all of this. My day will be better for it. And I sincerely wish the same for you.

Oct. 29, 1998

Those Old Triggers

By Laura L.

> *I had a vision yesterday of a quiet afternoon in a quiet bar, relaxing and sipping a couple of vodka tonics and flipping through a magazine with the television going quietly in the background and occasionally chatting with the bartender. – D.*

Yeah, sitting around at Borders bookstore with a cup of cafe latte doesn't quite have the same pleasure to it, does it? <g> Maybe in time…

You know, it's funny how we picture ourselves in these romanticized memories. Eight years ago, when my mother returned to the US, my sister, mother and I went to dinner at a wonderful French restaurant. There was a screw-up with our table, and we had to wait a couple hours to be seated. The restaurant also housed a jazz "club" so we went there. The music was great (live, of course), the ambiance of the place was seductive, and I was so very happy we had been able to convince the authorities that my mom REALLY needed to be allowed to leave England (whole 'nother story). At any rate, I was having the *de rigueur* Diet Pepsi, they were having wine, and all was well. From across the room, I spotted a couple -- both stunningly attractive, beautifully dressed, elegant in every way. The woman was holding a snifter of brandy to the light, and swirling it in the glass. That image was so compelling, I was beginning to make plans for my return to "normal" drinking (yeah right!).

Then I began to think about what the scene would be like if it was "me" instead of "her." Here's what I realized.

It would not be a snifter of brandy, it would be vodka -- and WAY more than one.

My beautiful dress would not cover up my running makeup, puffy eyes, and slurred speech. In fact, my dress would have been selected on the basis of how many people would be offended by it.

This would not have preceded or followed an elegant dinner, and there would be no live jazz, either. It would have been balls to the wall drinking, and the more "dangerous" the setting, the happier I would be.

My date would not have on a suit. In fact, my "date" would have been "discovered" after I had consumed five or more drinks.

My "date" and I would not be swirling on the dance floor, but would be fumbling and drunk in the dark. More than once, I found that my "date" for the night had relieved me of the contents of my wallet before leaving the apartment.

It's so easy for us to be led down the garden path of embellished memories. I have found it helpful to recall one moment, frozen in time, to recall. That moment is seeing the elegant couple, and knowing that woman would never be me. It is a waste of time for me to try to emulate her.

Besides, I have more fun being me -- sober.

Oct. 29, 1998

Roller Coaster Emotions

By Treena W.

Had a terrible day that ended a crappy week. This is how it all happened. Not sure if you all know it but I am diagnosed with Bipolar Disorder or as they sometimes call it, Manic Depression.

Basically what it means is one's emotions are like a roller coaster; one instant curled up in the fetal position in the corner not talking crying or even existing, contemplating suicide and how great it would be to feel a series of rounds from a submachine gun pierce your brain, and the next instant so intensely happy and powerful that you think you could easily become the President/Prime Minister/Pope/whatever and obtain world peace, and so hyper that you think you'll turn inside out, explode and shower your guts on everyone within a three mile radius.

Thankfully, there are medications for this condition. I have been on a cocktail of a couple of them for about 4 years, and they have saved my life. HOWEVER, since I've been sober, I've felt so empowered that I thought perhaps my depression was caused by the alcohol, and decided to try to "taper" my meds, without any doctor's advice. That started Monday. I decreased my dosage by half, thinking that if it caused a negative reaction, I could easily up my dosage back to where it should be. I should have known better, since I've tried this stunt before and it never got anything but negative results. But for some reason I keep thinking that since everything was different "pre-sobriety," that I can blame everything on drinking.

Not true. Tuesday, I began shopping. [...] The stores were crowded and cheerful, with Shitmas music playing nonstop. I thought I was enjoying it. I passed bar after bar, pub after pub, and as the day grew on, I realized I wasn't enjoying it at all. I was actually hoping that I would dislike it so much that I would give in and have a drink. But I didn't. [...]

Wednesday, I decided to venture back out [...] I went straight to Winners to look for a coat. I found the perfect one plus a hat and wore them out of the store, (after paying for them of course *g*).... Then I began my search through the electronic hell area on foot for the scanner. After zigzagging the street several times, writing down specs, warding off evil salespeople, passing by the beer store twice, liquor store and a "cute little" wine store, I finally narrowed it down to 2 choices of scanners. Then I had lunch at Wendy's (taco salad and a sprite) and called my husband with the options. We decided on one, and I trudged back over to the first store I had visited to make my purchase. I grabbed a cab home, satisfied and broke.

By this time the lack of medicine was kicking in and I was again craving large. It was a different kind of craving though. Not a physical "I want a drink now" kind of craving. It was more of a "I want to be normal" craving. It felt like if I could just have a choice to say "yes" or "no" to a drink, then I'd never want to get loaded again. Like, the pressure of never being able to drink again was pushing me to binge.

As ridiculous as it sounds, I had the idea that it was "binge or moderate".... Sobriety wasn't even a comfortable option. I felt like I was starting all over again, back to square one. Almost as if I had relapsed without the booze. Everything I had worked for in the last 30 days was gone. I felt as if I had just quit yesterday. To top it all off my ISP was down for 24 hours and I couldn't get back on here till around 10:30 today....

My husband came home and immediately knew something was up. So we talked. I balked, he talked, I balked some more....yadayadayada.... It helped. I've realized that being and staying sober (at this point for me) is like walking a tightrope. It's such a delicate balance of feelings and ideas. So much control involved. I can't let my guard down for one instant. If I do, that "dumb brain" comes back and tries to justify everything I know is wrong. I realized that tapering my meds is a bad idea too. I'm going back to my regular dosage immediately.

I also realized that I have to get back to "just today"... in order to help make tomorrow a good sober day. I have to keep working. I thought I was through the worst but I was wrong. Four weeks ain't much, I'm learning, and there's still a long way for me to go. I figured out (again) through our discussion that I really cannot moderate. That it really isn't worth it. That really all I was wanting was a binge. And that I have to be strong and keep fighting it, but I have to allow myself room for the slip, otherwise the pressure gets to be too much and I get "tired of recovering" which leads to all these thoughts of moderation. By giving myself that room, I'm basically saying, "as long as I do my best then it will be ok".... It takes the pressure off, and I can concentrate on staying sober instead of wanting to give up on it.

This might not make any sense to you all, then again maybe it does. The idea of "giving myself room to slip-up" probably sounds ridiculously dangerous to anyone who is trying to stay sober, but once I realized that the fear of "f-ing up" was what was causing my stress, and making me tired, I felt really good about saying "my best is all I can do and if I do f up, then I get back up and try again." I know now that trying moderation is way more dangerous than risking a one-time binge.

I was wondering what the difference between f'ing up at abstinence and f'ing up at moderation was if the result is the same — abstinence, and my husband explained it quite well. If I try moderating, sure it could work for some time but eventually I'm going to binge again and it could be a year down the road. At that time I'd have to try abstaining again, and it would be a lot harder to start over at that point than if I just f-up while trying to abstain. Not to mention the other downfalls of trying to moderate. This is the best reason I have heard yet. Who, knows, maybe I'm setting myself up for a slip, but I know that the ideas of moderation are gone and that's in tune with my master plan: abstinence....

That's all for now … thanks for listening to a pretty screwy girl half way (but not going all the way) into a bipolar episode...:-)...

Nov. 4, 1998

Sobriety Has Its Own Momentum

By Diane J.

> *<I've come to the realization that this alcoholism is something that will never go away. There will never be a day when I'll "get better".- M.>*

I'm glad you posted. I wouldn't wish this on anyone else either, absolutely not -- but since you and I and others on this list seem to share "this," perhaps we can help each other with it.

You write: "There will never be a day when I will 'get better.'" That was an important and painful realization for me, the outcome of struggling to "control," to "learn," to "limit," to "keep the drinking down to once a (fill in the rapidly decreasing blank--semester, month, week, only after 7:00 PM, not before 5:00, never in the afternoon...)" over and over and over and over, with varying and wearying lengths of partial success leading to total failure AGAIN.

You would think the sheer stupefying repetition would have taught me something (I personally think the wheel of samsara is BEST depicted in a "robot drinking" cycle--laugh). I didn't begin to get free of it until I understood the true lesson in the failures to "learn how." The true lesson is that, when it comes to alcohol, I CANNOT learn.

In all those years of trying to learn, I never once succeeded for very long, every clever plan and powerful resolution overwhelmed by the sheer drive to keep drinking, which easily found plausible excuses for doing so and rationales for trying the NEXT clever plan to "learn" to "keep the drinking down to …." There is nothing to learn except that there is nothing you can learn. Just let go. Drop your end of the rope and the desire to drink will -- EVENTUALLY, SLOWLY, INTERMITTENTLY-- drop its end and begin to vanish.

The longer you stay completely stopped (and I didn't believe this either, but it turns out to be strangely and wonderfully true) the less effort it takes to STAY stopped. Sobriety has its own momentum.

But in the beginning, and for a longish time, it takes a great deal of work and effort (I found) to KEEP stopped. So why not let go of all the work it takes to repeat failing to learn and put the energy into whatever tools work for you to stay stopped long enough for the struggle to begin to lessen? As long as you stay in the tug of war, by continuing to get drunk sporadically, you will never get to the "effortless" part you want. Or at least I couldn't.

I would hardly say, even now, that it's effortless, but it is easier. And less exhausting, and less self-punishing. And leaves me room to put some energies OUT of myself and into positive change for myself and I hope for others. So let go. Just lose. Admit defeat, and there never was a war (smile). And put the energy where you can learn something valuable. Take care.

Nov. 5, 1998

AWOL From 12-Step Treatment

By Michael H.

Hi everybody. I'm back on the list from treatment and am proud to say that I lasted exactly 1 hour and 15 min in their program. I left so fast I even left my books on the desk in the classroom.

The year is currently 1998. We have pretty much decided that chemical addictions are genetic and/or cognitive behavior problems and not some metaphysical plot by some divine entity to lead us to spirituality. Although I agree that AA has helped many, I believe that its dominance in the medical field is not only improper, but unethical in this day and age.

I have been treated for many things in my life and not one doctor has ever told me to pray over a broken rib, pneumonia, Rocky Mountain spotted fever, depression or even the flu. Why should I have to do it for (in my case) this genetic disorder?

Big Books no longer belong on treatment wards. They belong in the Chaplain's office with the rest of the religious tracts.

When I want spirituality, I go to church where my Reverend does a fine job with those issues.

Thank you

Michael H.

Hiding from the 12 steppers in the woods of Tennessee.

Nov. 8, 1998

The Sky Didn't Fall In

By Diane J.

I have to tell you quickly about the conversation I just had with my "Saturday boss" here at this very boring phone job that I've had for a few weeks to try to get out of debt (laugh). I was "golden girl" this morning -- showed up, unlike 2 of the other people scheduled, had arranged my schedule to cover hours next week, got my calls made, hit my quota. Had spotted, in her office, Web screen obviously up on computer. Went in to cover the office phone for lunch as arranged and asked, rather timidly, "Could I use that to do some web mail?"

"Sure, sure -- it's a flat fee account anyway." Yippee! Open my mail. Screen after screen of [SOSmail]-headed messages that I haven't gotten to in two days. Rapture.

"Is that a mailing list or something? What's that?"

Oh shit. She hasn't left yet. Oh SHIT....

"What?" (Great response, Diane....)

"That. SOSMail....." pointing over my shoulder.

Ummmmm … oh no. Ummm .... Save Our Souls, Ralph Reed's new group? Sell Out Successfully, the mailing list for greedy Yuppies? … Ummm … what the fuck, I hate this job anyway....

"It stands for Secular Organizations for Sobriety." That oughta kill THIS conversation….

Look of concern and then lightbulb. "I had an alcoholic boyfriend once. Do you have one too?"

Oh GAWD....yeah, that's IT, I'm little Florrie Nightingale trying to stand by mah man … nah, I've never done this before and I got this far….

"Ummm … actually, I belong to it."

Clunk. Hey, you know, I can quit right NOW, I don't have to wait till you come back from lunch….

"Oh." Pause. "How did you find out--you know?"

Ummmm … well, the DTs were kind of a clue? Ummmm … well, when they locked me up for 'treatment,' I guessed ... ummmm ....

"You figure it out."

"Oh." Look of sad puzzlement. "You know, he was a

really nice guy, I mean, he was really great ... but he just couldn't stop drinking, you know?"

Oh yeah. I know.

"Do you go to AA meetings and stuff?"

Deep breath. "No, I didn't like AA. That's why I joined SOS."

"He used to go to meetings, but he just couldn't stop drinking." Shaking head. "But he was a really nice guy. Hey, I kind of put you on the spot, I'm sorry, forget it, OK?"

"OK."

"I'll be back at 1:30 and you have the new survey forms ready, OK?"

"OK, thanks."

Wow. So I still have the stupid job (which means I gotta go collate the survey forms now). Hey, I actually told somebody the truth and the sky didn't fall in. What an interesting universe this has turned out to be ... (laugh).

But thank you everyone again for being there. I don't think I'll forget the look on her face as she kept repeating, "he was a really nice guy...." Or the really nice guy whose name I don't even know who kept going to the meetings and drinking...

Thanks. Many thanks for being there.

Nov. 14, 1998

The Phantom Strikes Again

By Ward T.

< *My first hand experience with AA spans nearly 3 decades. I have seen during that time a significant change in the organization, a move away from a general benevolent tolerance under the influence of the then existing "oldtimers" who had been around in the early years of AA. Today's "oldtimers" have come of age in an established mainstream organization. There is very little tolerance for anything that varies from what they know as the one true way. – B.* >

I went to an AA meeting the other night and while speaking ended up giving a sort of farewell speech. I explained how I wanted to continue in AA as a supplement to SOS but the cold shoulders I've been receiving lately have led me to drop out totally.

I explained how surprised I was at a lot of the old timers and even newbies at how closed-minded they were to an alternative. Recovery should be our main goal, I continued, and that AA'ers should review all the new alternatives and educate themselves on them so if another person like myself comes to the program you can offer alternatives.

I explained how disappointed I was in the lack of support. I guess it can be expected. As I spoke more there was chattering and some chuckling developing in the back. After I finished and introduced the next speaker some robots clapped (I know it wasn't because my speech was uplifting) and several others including my sponsor didn't.

AA'ers always spoke to me about my fair weather friends when I was drinking -- put down the drink and then see if they still come around. It's so hypocritical now that I'm working my recovery in another direction. I've been hanging with an AA'er for over 5 years and we became pretty close. He was a very good friend of my family. Since I started to work SOS he's been scarce and now I find out he organized a golf trip (we were close golfing partners) of AA'ers and didn't even tell me about it. So much for that.

I'm done with AA. For my own therapy I went out last night to three AA meetings in my area and distributed over

100 flyers under windshields. I made sure I went early to catch the beginners meetings. It felt good to distribute the materials, I feel like such a rebel. I should get a costume with a cape and mask: The Phantom of SOS strikes again! Nah -- too weird.

Nov. 14, 1998

Here Today

By Steve C.

> *I was just wondering how others deal with the feelings that you know you're going to be on the planet and then gone? - C.*

Well, since you asked.... When I die, I'll rot, or I'll be cremated, or I'll be buried, or what not, but I won't be gone. I'm a part of the earth. I was born on the earth (so they tell me), I consume what is grown and raised here for my own existence, and I will return back to the earth. I'm quite content thinking of myself as being fertilizer.

As far as my consciousness is concerned, the electrical system that makes up my mind will probably still be around, in the soil, in the sky, maybe just static electricity. I don't know. However, I can be sure that my physical part will remain and be used by the creatures still upon the earth in some way shape or form.

Whatever our life force or consciousness is, a form of energy, or just electrical impulses, will not be destroyed. If I understand physics correctly, the worst that can happen is that it is converted from energy to matter, or from matter to energy, but it won't just be gone.

The me as I know myself will be gone, but I'll still be around, I just won't know it, and I'll probably be distributed all over the place. I guess we all go to pieces at some time or the other. But I think its gratifying to know that I've been with the earth for as long as its been around, and I'll be with the earth as long as the earth exists, and even if our fair and precious planet explodes someday, I'll still be a part of the universe, maybe just space dust, but still around. We're all immortal.

When I'm dead and decomposed, maybe I'll be a part of some other creature, or plant, or thing, maybe even just poop. But even in death, I'll be a part of life, and if I'm not a part of life, at least I'll be a part of something, maybe just one of my sodium atoms on an asteroid.

It makes me really want to stay sober to enjoy my current conscious life status all the more. It really is amazing that I find myself in my current life form to experience my body, my mind, my planet and my universe to the greatest extent possible. If nothing else, I can just wonder at the marvel of it, and I take great comfort in knowing that even if I think I'm not a part of it, I really am. How can I possibly ever be detached from it?

Okay okay, I'll shut up, but you asked.

Nov. 15, 1998

That "One Last Binge"

By Diane J.

> *Why do I keep thinking that I have a binge coming up? Why do I feel I deserve "one last binge?" I'm actually looking forward to it. Not all the time but it does enter my mind occasionally. Yesterday was the worst so far. I was determined to get beer. On one hand I feel totally in control and then it all escapes me and here I am planning my next drunk. I still feel like I need one more binge ... and I can't seem to get it out of my head. Any input appreciated. – T.*

I sort of managed to convince myself I needed "one last binge" A LOT -- I was one of those people who was always going to quit "next week" when "things' aren't quite so "hectic" and I can REALLY REALLY REALLY ... oh, what's the point (laugh)? I never quite DID it. If I had a dollar for every "last bottle" I ever bought I could be spending this weekend on a beach somewhere ... (laugh).

And when I finally "started to stop" (stutter sobriety, I think -- laugh) the "one last binge" idea kept coming back at me, too. I finally had "one last binge" last fall. Ummm.... I coulda skipped delirium tremens, I really coulda.

Let me tell you something about that idea about "one last binge," OK? It's not going to go away for a while after you stop drinking totally, unfortunately.... Even after that last disastrous binge, well into my first few months of sobriety, I'd find myself thinking about having "a really really really last binge ... better this time (laugh), of course…." That's the addiction talking, I think.

Part of getting sober is learning to talk back to it. Put a little reality into those fantasies. Jennifer gave you wonderful advice when she wrote about "thinking the binge all the WAY through." How good would that binge BE, really? Isn't the fact that you're planning one, even though you mean to QUIT for good, proof that there's something wrong with your drinking, that it's about time to get it over with? Same thing with the moderation idea, probably, unfortunately.

You DO have "two brains," sort of, at the moment: there's the sensible, smart, realistic woman who KNOWS that the drinking's been out of control and the stuff is bad for her -- ah, but then there's the woman who's used to drinking a hell of a lot and CRAVES more alcohol and finds the idea of sobriety pretty scary and uncomfortable.

Treat it like a voice in your ear if that helps (I called mine "my addict:" argue with it. Don't let it push you around. Isn't it, for example, interesting that the little voice is suggesting BOTH bingeing and drinking "moderately?" Now why would THAT be (laugh)? REAL moderate drinkers don't sit around planning their next drunk, at least not in my experience.

What that little voice wants is back AT IT -- and it takes some willingness to be uncomfortable and sit through craving to get it to shut up. If you feed it it just comes back even louder.

You write:

> *Perhaps it's because I'm not educated enough on the science of my addiction. If only I had some scientific proof that I definitely can never drink another drop without falling back into the old patterns, then I could give up on those menacing thoughts that enter my mind on a daily basis*

Good luck (laugh). You can always find somebody, somewhere, who wrote something that with enough concentration and imagination and (possibly five or six drinks in you) you can construe as being "proof" that maybe maybe maybe there's a little little little possibility that you might possibly possibly be in the tiny percentage of people who-- GET TO DRINK AGAIN!

The question is how much pain has drinking already caused you? And, if you weren't hooked on the stuff in some way, would you EVER believe the pleasure it gives could be worth THAT MUCH pain?

These are tough days, I know. Glad to see you posting and hang in there. Keep arguing with yourself! Take care.

Nov. 17, 1998

We Need More Choices

By Jenny S.

> *The business of 12 Step theology being forced upon people by the supposedly secular institutions of courts and health care is a appalling ,and has the potential of really fucking up your head. – R.*

Thanks for giving me something to think about. Why is it that the courts don't offer any choice when it comes to mandated counseling/recovery meetings?

I know someone that was told by the courts to go to AA meetings and counseling. Had she been sent to somewhere other than AA maybe she wouldn't be so determined to destroy herself now. I really believe their insistence that she was a powerless person, and all that focus on the past made her feel even worse about herself and sent her even deeper into her addictions.

Everyone is an individual, and should be treated that way. There is no one way that is right for everyone. And being told that if you don't recover in AA you will never recover at all is not going to help anyone.

Nov. 20, 1998

Straight to Blackout

By Steve C.

I remember when I was around 19 or 20, I almost beat the hell out of my girlfriend's father. I broke a few dishes, yelled and screamed at him, and finally, after he called the cops, I split. After about a year of sneaking around behind his back with his daughter, he decided to allow me to come back into his house. At dinner that very evening, he offered me a drink. I said no thanks. He said, it's okay to drink, you don't have to quit drinking, just don't drink so much.

I remember my kids crying to me, telling me that it was okay to drink, just don't get drunk. My wife told me the same thing, numerous times. I've been told the same thing by numerous friends: just be careful. Take a taxi home; don't drink so much, etc. A totaled car, a couple of motorcycle accidents, a bike wreck, countless fights, one DUI, six or seven other arrests, and several incidents of vandalism and home-wrecking, never convinced me to quit trying.

For over 30 years, I have always gone overboard. I could never consistently control it, and thinking back on it, this was the cause of many negative feelings about myself. What kind of asshole am I. Why did I always go till I passed out. I almost always went straight to blackout, and almost always found myself wondering what I had done, and what had happened.

Well, the answer finally came to me. It was the fact that I took a drink. I can't remember how many times I went to the bar with extremely pressing business or personal items to take care of that day, that I just blew off. No contact with the world for another day. Waking up to find numerous messages on my answering machine wondering where I was, why I dropped an appointment, or where some work product was.

It took me thirty years of starting with the best of intentions, and going straight to blackout that finally convinced me to just not get started. I remember my DUI back in '91, taking the state mandated alcohol treatment program where I learned that alcohol affects the judgment centers of the mind.

Kewel, I thought. I just won't drink when I have pressing things to do. Well, that plan didn't even work, because it didn't allow me enough opportunities to get drunk. I figured, I'd only drink while camping or fishing. Only drink where my behavior didn't have the potential to harm anyone else. Well, it was a big problem. I never did move to a cave or to the streets where maybe I wouldn't have to worry about anyone else.

I don't get into a discussion with drinking friends about alcoholism, I just tell them I quit drinking. Period, end of story, give me a Coke. I don't discuss it with non-drinkers either, never did like or trust them. No matter what anybody else tells me, I just say no. I must, for my sake, the sake of my kids, the sake of my marriage, the sake of my business, for the sake of my friends, and for the sake of society, just say no to the first drink. I finally know and have a deep, deep, deep conviction that I can't control my drinking. I never have, I never could, and I never will. I never, I think, even wanted just one drink. I wanted or maybe needed to get drunk. This need manifests itself in a million different ways, but in the end, all I need to do is control my right arm. I just don't hoist it to my lips, no matter what, no matter what anybody says, no matter what anybody does, and no matter how the rest of the world handles it.

Sure, this left a lot of weird feelings at first. I had great emotional difficulty at first. I'm not sure why, and once in a great while, I still get a strong craving. This list, meetings, reading literature, long walks, playing with the dog, playing with the kids, working, learning, and all kinds of other stuff now occupies most of my life. But, I have complete control over my arm that I will lose once I get started drinking. I'm mortally afraid of even trying to take one drink because it was just too damned hard to get to where I am today. I really don't think I could or would come back. Sure, many others have, but I'm really afraid to even try. The appeal of drunkenness is too great for me. I love to be drunk, I love the feeling of it, and I have gotten drunk at the expense of every thing else that was important in my life. I don't want to die with alcohol on my breath.

I find it is just easier for me to manage it without using it. It really is a far more simple method for me, and one that gives me a more positive outlook. At remaining completely sober, I have been successful. It removes me from the constant battles that I always lost trying to control it. I can win the war by just not engaging the enemy. I know I can't drink now. Never now. Maybe next week, but not now.

Nov. 21, 1998

The Ultimate Message

By Treena W.

While lying in bed last night, after reading the "keepers" from the SOS page, and trying to fall asleep, I was once again overcome by the confusion and questions on the topic of moderate drinking: "what if?" "why can't I?" etc. etc. As the thoughts, voices and ideas performed their barbaric, ritual dance in my head, I came to an amazing realization. It entered my mind as subtly as a whisper and hit my brain with the power of a thousand jackhammers. I can't remember exactly what thoughts produced the revelation, as they left my mind as quickly and subtly as they had entered it. It doesn't really matter how the message got there. All I know is that the ultimate message finally came through. The message was:

"Don't drink, no matter what!!!!!!!! Free yourself. Sobriety is better. No matter what. Nothing compares to it."

I've got a lot of work to do to maintain this attitude, and a long way to go before I'm 100% comfortable with it, but, after 18 days, I finally have found the answer. It was there all along. Thank you.

Nov. 23, 1998

Evil Boss and Sweet Me

By Rex A.

During the past year, I have had occasion to spend more time in bars and other drinking situations than in the entire previous 13 years of sobriety combined. And I have discovered, very much to my pleasure, that the desire or temptation to drink simply isn't there.

If the venue is a noisy, smoky bar, most of my attention is focused on trying to protect my poor, sweet nervous system from the loud music and cigarette smoke. I hate, with a capital "H," shouting to try to communicate a few words to someone, and then straining and straining to try to make out their answer. I don't know whether I am deaf or what, but I watch the other people around me appearing to go through the motions of conversation, and I just don't get it. In any event, once I go into one of those places, my goal is to take care of "business" and then get the hell out. When I get home, my clothes all reek of cigarette smoke. What a turn off! In that sense, nothing could be better for or more reinforcing of my sobriety!

BTW, I don't recommend that you try this if you are in early sobriety! Stay away from "slippery places," for awhile anyway. Please.

As to restaurants and dinners where other people are drinking, it is just a non-issue, I don't even notice or pay attention to the fact that people around me are drinking booze ... until and unless someone has too much and becomes unpleasantly drunk. But that is really a separate issue. And, as I have shared before, I don't feel at all awkward, apologetic, or defensive in asserting the fact that I don't drink. No one has ever pushed the issue with me, but if they did, that person would be permanently scratched off my list, and I wouldn't spend 20 seconds mourning the loss of the relationship.

My former (evil) boss and I had dinner on a couple of occasions. It was funny. We had exactly, precisely the same conversation both times, it was like we were reading from a script.

EVIL BOSS: Would you like some wine?

SWEET ME: No thanks!

EVIL BOSS: Don't you drink?
SWEET ME: Nope.
EVIL BOSS: Nothing?
SWEET ME: No.
EVIL BOSS: You are a teetotaler?
SWEET ME: Yes.
EVIL BOSS: Strictly?
SWEET ME: Yes, strictly.

Clearly, she wanted more of an explanation from me, and just as clearly, she was not going to get it. And it's not because I am shy or embarrassed about disclosing being alcoholic. It is just that I have a very clear sense of "propriety" and of boundaries. And it this instance, it was none of her damn business, and nothing would have been served by getting into a discussion about it.

Let me just state a principle from C[ognitive] B [ehavioral] T[herapy]: You are under no obligation to answer anyone's question(s) unless you are testifying in front of the grand jury. Of course, there are diplomatic ways to finesse, avoid, evade and refuse to answer that are less offensive than others. You can readily learn them. But the principle stands. Just because someone asks you a question, does not mean you are compelled to answer, or to answer meaningfully. Naturally, some people may be a little irritated when you don't cough up the information they are trying to get out of you, but that's their problem. It is your prerogative what you choose to share and who you choose to share it with, and that's the end of it.

Nov. 27, 1998

The Power I Have To Deal With

By Dale H.

At the root of any lasting sobriety (in my experience) lies a fundamental self-confidence, usually a product of boosted self-esteem through personal successes.

Whenever a person relies solely on a "power" outside himself, failure is likely to occur. I've seen it within and outside AA.

I had to come to realize that the one person/thing/power/"being" I have to deal with, and come to grips with, is myself.

With a lot of help from other alcoholics and in turn an ability to share my hopes and dreams with another alcoholic I have found joy in life, a joy I never knew existed while drinking.

Well, enough of this sermon ... have fun!

Dec. 1, 1998

The Price Goes Up

By Jim S.

> *Perhaps if I get some stories I can relate to it might help put an end to this confusion I have towards moderation. – T.*

If you take my post as a testimonial to the merits of "trying" it again please don't do it. Not worth the trouble. In my sober attempts over the past 3 or so years I've "made it" 6, 8, 2, 4 months respectively. Toss in a grouping of a few weeks and/or days now and then. Each time guess what? The pain is the same. The shame is the same. The disgust and self-loathing is the same. The only difference from episode to episode is the price increases -- meaning both retail prices and personal prices. Each time just a bit more of the esteem goes, a scosh more cognitive brain power, a huge physical price tag.

The mind is a very, very, strange beast indeed. It will tell me just what it is telling you, that you can do it. News flash to me ... no I can't and I would only speculate -- but you can't either. Moderation? Well, I can tell you from my experience that it does not work. I most likely (given past history) may once again make that foolish decision. I hope not. Christ I hope not.

Dec. 6, 1998

Amazingly Enough

By Jennifer S.

> *One of the things that came up this week at my counselor's was the fact that I am trying to get away from myself. – D.*

This came up for me several times. I was told, "The problem with trying to get away from yourself is, no matter where you go, there you are."

When I realized how true this statement was it was kind of scary. I knew I'd have to deal with me sooner or later. In my case, I would drink or use drugs to escape from my life. Problem was, my life wasn't what I was trying to get away from. It was me.

And no matter how drunk or high I got I was still there. I was there before I drank, while I was getting drunk, and while I was dealing with the consequences of what I did drunk. No matter how hard I tried I just couldn't get rid of myself.

So after years of trying, I decided to get to know me. There's a lot I don't like. And I'm working on those things. But there is a lot I love! I never would have known that if I didn't stop drinking and using.

> *If you wait around until you "feel better" before you stop drinking, you are probably going to have a long, painful wait. – R.*

Very true. I wasted two years waiting to "feel better." I thought if I just waited until my marriage was better, until we had money, until I got the house organized, until the kids started school and I could go back to work … etc. I thought that then, I wouldn't have to drink. When my life was perfect I wouldn't *need* to drink.

I've learned two things about this:

1. Life is not now, and will never be, "perfect."
2. Quitting drinking IS what makes you feel better.

Amazingly enough <g> after the alcohol was gone from my life, so were many of the problems I was drinking over.

Dec. 7, 1998

People Who Understand

By Larry D.

> *Tomorrow I'll have 90 days sober, and I'm glad to be able to share that with all of you, because it doesn't mean that much to the people in my life who haven't been down this particular road. – S.*

TOOT! TOOT! That's really great. When I was at 90 days, I think the strongest emotion I felt, even stronger than the absolute unfairness that of all the people who need it so bad, I CAN'T DRINK, was how awful it was that nobody appreciated how hard it was to quit drinking: not my wife, not people at work, not my students -- they all expected me to just behave normally, with no temper tantrums, crying spells, foul moods, or other outbursts. A month later, I was finally desperate enough that I started attending AA meetings (no SOS then), and whatever their other failings might have been, it felt really good to finally be around people who understood what I was going through.

I think that the #1 thing that groups like ours can do is to offer that understanding; we know what it is like for J. to be struggling at 72 hours, and what it is like for you to face a 90-day birthday during the holiday season.

So congratulations, and thank you for your 90 days -- every day that you don't drink our group is that much stronger, and you have that much more to share with us.

Hey, I like that thought -- each and every day that we all hang in there and don't drink, our group is 160 sober-days stronger. Who says sobriety must be earned one day at a time?

Dec. 8, 1998

I'd Just Rather Be Me

By Bill McD.

Howdy Everyone. A few Mozart-induced thoughts of a gray and drizzly morning:

> *"to be nobody-but-yourself-in a world which is doing its best, night and day, to make you everybody else - means to fight the hardest battle which any human being can fight; and never stop fighting." (e.e. cummings)*

This appears on my "Zen a day" calendar for last Monday, and I have been thinking about it, on and off, for the rest of the week. It seems to me that cummings, while addressing a more general, "condition of man" kind of thing, may as well have been speaking directly to those of us fighting addiction.

After all, we are all of us on a search for self, something we touched on last week a couple of times, if memory serves. All of us, to some degree or another, lived lives that were not our own, in which we followed the dictates of alcohol and/or drugs and, all too often, the whims and fickle vagaries of some rather questionable companions. And at some point, we all decided that this was not a healthy way to be. So we have this great commonality, but at the same time, we are more diverse. We were, I think, much more alike when we were still using, and what a sorry lot I daresay we were.

Sober, we have a diversity of opinion which is rich and lively, sometimes fun and sometimes angry, by turns profound and mind-numbingly plebeian. All of this is good, and a far cry from the sameness we once exhibited: Thinking ourselves "terminally unique," to borrow from AA, we were the proverbial dime-a-dozen. Every barroom had a number of us in there, talking shit and meaning it and forgetting it and returning to hold forth some more the next day. Too many living rooms had one of us, watching bad television, cursing our luck in the world and dreading what the next day was going to bring down on us. Cheers!

What binds us now, it seems to me, is something greater even than our common fight for sobriety. Knowing what we were, seeing, possibly for the first time, what each of us has the potential to become, we feel a need to encourage the growth in each other, even when it means we know we're gonna argue, sometimes even viciously. We are helping each other to become individuals, something we were, for the most part, excruciatingly bad at before. I think we see this mostly in newcomers, who are still fighting the idea that maybe their old "friends" aren't the best people in the world to hang out with anymore, that maybe they shouldn't have whiskey in the house or go to happy hour, that the "just one more" bug is poisonous and horrible and wrong. The using society is a hard one to leave behind, for the very simple reason that we got a sense of self, however warped and mangled, from that society.

As we move on toward sobriety, we find that our minds and our souls feel lighter and more free; we become more capable of looking critically at things which once were not only acceptable but even desirable, things that now seem to be stupid and harmful. As we explore that mental/emotional freedom, that new-found critical ability, we slowly, slowly, discover who and what we are.

And it is not easy. It is the most difficult thing most of us will ever do. Because there are some demons in there, deep in our pasts, which have shaped us, and they are not pretty to look at. But they are us, to some degree, and as such have to be accepted or killed off and replaced. We can do that, now, either one. This is a part of becoming "nobody-but-yourself," I think. When we were a part of that drinking/using "everybody else," our arguments were loud and crude and meaningless; that which we cannot remember is not a valid lesson, or a valid point. And they were the same arguments, night after night, pounded on again and again because we were so woefully misunderstood and the world just didn't get it. I myself had EVERY SINGLE PROBLEM IN THE UNIVERSE SOLVED. Absolutely true. 'Course, I have no idea what my solutions were, but I'm sure they were great.

Somehow, I think I'd just rather be me. Wrong, right, whatever. At least now I know that if I piss somebody off, or if I make them think or laugh, I'll remember, tomorrow, what I said, and know that I meant it. And that it was me doing the talking and thinking, not thirteen Bass Ales and a multicolored shooter with a very strange name….

2/28/99

The best thing that happened

By Joy H.

There are forces out there messing with me big time.... Yesterday, started off morning bad with various little things -- I woke up with a stiff neck (rare for me), got an electrical shock on the way to work, got to work to process month-end and all the copy machines broke on me, one at a time. Then found out IRS decided to seize my refund this year because of two ex husband's returns. At lunch I got a phone call from the Police Dept that my 17-yr. old son was picked up for truancy (missed 13 days of school) and he had marijuana on him (he's living with his father right now). Then, when leaving police dep't., my car died. Had $60 in bank, thank goodness only a battery, so had enough to cover it. Then I get home to find a letter in the mail stating I owe a finance company $12,583 for a voluntary repo on a vehicle last year. When I went to turn in to bed, went to bathroom and it was the coup de grace, perfect end to perfect day — NO toilet paper! Not sure exactly what kept me from falling off the wagon, but that was the best thing that happened to me yesterday. I didn't drink. But frankly, don't know how much more I can take. So for all of us, when we have bad days, just remember to tap that inner strength and DONT DRINK NO MATTER WHAT!

3/2/99

It Just Keeps Getting Better

By Bill Mc.D.

Howdy Everyone:

Some reflections on a cold wants-to-snow kind of a Sunday morning.

Next week is my nine-months. I know a lot of people don't count their sober days/weeks, but I still find it helpful; it keeps things in perspective for me. Next Sunday, all things being equal, I will have been sober for exactly three percent as long as I drank. That's the kind of startling and encouraging stat that really helps keep a body going. Okay, that's a little depressing, maybe. It's more encouraging, perhaps, to realize that, as of next Sunday, I will have sober time amounting to 10.4% of Cal Ripken's now-infamous streak. Yeah, that's better....

A lot of things have changed in that pipsqueak amount of time. For one thing, I spend Sunday mornings reflecting on stuff like the previous week, contemplating the upcoming one, and engaging in other quiet pursuits like listening to music, reading the paper, and "updating my journal." (Hell, I still remember when it was called "keeping a diary," and it was something my little sister did, and was inordinately proud of....)

This morning I am also contemplating taking in a movie later with a very dear friend, providing the weather is kind. For too long, Sunday mornings started at 10:30 with a quick shower 'n' puke so that I could make opening time at one of the local watering holes. Sundays were a time of reflection only if "what the hell did I do last night?" is considered reflection.

My refrigerator has food in it. Food that requires actual preparation, beyond hitting the "reheat" button on my microwave. Food that might, god help me, actually be good for me, prepared properly. Okay, no real danger in that....

I find that I face up to things better than I used to. If it was ugly, I ran away, basically trying to wait it out. Not the smartest move ever: ugly things take root and get bigger when we try to wait 'em out. They're more patient than we are.

I am more patient with people, generally speaking. I still have very little patience with an obvious moron, but I'm also finding that those are fewer and farther between than I apparently thought previously.

I care more than I used to. I like to think I've always been a pretty nice guy at heart, but the only thing I really cared about, of course, was the next round. I have found that it's real hard to get that worked up over cranberry juice....

I think I act more like a friend now. (That of course is also made easier by virtue of the simple fact that there are fewer people I call "friend" now. I suspect that I found it real hard to get worked up over the problems of someone I just drank with every other Tuesday or whatever. Which, of course, is why the whole "bar friendship" thing is so flimsy. Everybody is worrying more about the next drink than what your perceived problem du jour might be.)

And I get through a lot of weird things without drinking. Lately, I get through them without thinking about drinking for the most part.

There are any number of other things that have changed as well, but I gotta save something for the big "1." Let's see, that'll be 4% of the time I drank. Or 13.87% of Cal's streak. It just keeps getting better, don't it?

Pax.

3/14/99

How Far I Have Come

By Sy S.

Hi to everyone! I was three on Friday!! I would have written then, but the mail server I subscribe to went down. I have had my ups and downs, but my quality of life has changed out of all proportion!!!

I still WELCOME each new day, gone is the dread that each new day brought with it when I was drinking, no more sky about to fall on my head, no more DT's, and those rats tails I kept seeing everywhere (you know the ones!).

No more of that little man hitting me over the head with a lump hammer each morning. No more hiding away, no sitting in out-of-the way places to drink alone, no more of looking at other people and wondering if I could lead a normal life.

I never thought I'd make it, but life does not stop, it carries on.

Hang in there, don't ever take your eyes off of that Priority: Keep Sober.

Nothing is ever worth going back to that dark lonely landscape, littered with the tortured corpses of millions who didn't make it. I see the horizon, but I don't aim for it, I enjoy the landscape around me, I walk my path, there are days when I can look back and see a clear view, and see how far I have come....

3/27/99

Out of Town In a Motel

By Joe B.

Hi all, I just went through the out-of-town-stay-in-a-motel thing for work. My boss and I went out for dinner and I had Coke while he polished off at least 6 Corbins and water. It's a new job (3 weeks) and I've mentioned it several times when the conversation got to drinking that I haven't done that in 10 months now.

No big deal when we went for cocktails beforehand, he ordered his and said “You don't drink, do you?” to me as I ordered my Coke. "Not anymore" was all I could think of, but it must have been enough to get the message across because it never entered the conversation again.

On the way to find the hotel after our customer call was done and he was mentioning having a few drinks someplace and then getting something to drink, I had the strongest urge to just have a few I have ever had in a long long time. 'What the heck, we're out of town, no one will ever know, etc.' was raging through my head.

Then when I got my room there was this nice little 2-glass complimentary bottle of Gallo sitting there. I thought about drinking it for a while, then changed my mind and decided to steal it instead and show my girlfriend what a hellian I am! I gave it to her, it fit nicely almost to the top of a large wine tumbler and she drank half and left the rest sitting there!

I don't believe I have ever done that in my life, if it's opened it needs drank, right? Instead it got poured out the next morning and I felt a tiny satisfaction that I'd passed some sort of test again.

I'll be on the road a lot in this new job, so I'm so glad I was able to fight off that initial intense urge to just go ahead and have a few with the boss since we are outta town. Setting that precedent right off the bat will make it easier for the next time I'm sitting in a hotel room looking at the wine or 50 mls of booze with no one to know but myself.

Another point that went through my head was that if I did drink a few I'd have a hard time telling you all about it, and I have enough going through my head with the new job to have to worry about anything new.

4/17/99

My Brain Said "Yuck"

By Bill McD.

Went to Lynchburg, VA on a business deal; this pretty much killed off the week. It was also the longest period of time I have lived in a hotel room "on my own" since I quit drinking. I was with two of my installers, both of whom at least know my history, even if they weren't witness to it.

For the most part, things were okay, but the little bastard did speak up a couple of times. The old refrain of "it's been a long and sweaty day and now it's time for a beer" was sung a time or two. It really is quite an enchanting song, when heard at the right-or wrong-time....

So, while my two traveling companions willingly headed for the Siren song, I did an Odysseus thing and plugged my ears by staying in the hotel room and reading.

Interesting thing, though: One night I was, in fact, out with the two of 'em. We were sitting at a table in this place called Mudpuppy's; they were drinking Heineken and I was drinking ginger ale/cranberry. Playing trivia, so my attention was focused on the TV screen. Because of where he had put it down, at one point I picked up Mike's bottle o'beer instead of my own drink.

Didn't drink from it, or really come close. I realized almost at once that I had grabbed the wrong thing. What was interesting about this "event" was the feelings and thoughts that went through me like a freight train, all at once: The bottle felt at home in my hand and the little bastard was yelling, "Awright, dude!" My brain shut down for just a second, deafened by LB's roar. I looked at the comfortable-feeling bottle. My brain came back online and *immediately* said, "Yuck."

Honest to whatever. My brain said, "yuck."

This was one of the cooler moments of the past ten months, if you ask me. I said "yuck" to -- this is the killer part -- A BEER. I used to live for the stuff, breathe it, sleep it, dream it.

As I have said in some post or other, my dreams usually have nothing to do with drinking anymore, but if drinking is "mentioned" it's always me *not* doing it. And now it seems that I've gotten to the point where if I do think about it, it kinda disgusts me.

This is good, I think. Good because it means that I have accepted the fact -- and it is a fact -- that alcohol and I don't get along real well, in the long run. So, yeah, it does happen after a while and life marches cheerily on. [...]

4/17/99

Sorting Through the Rubble

By Dee K.

My husband and I basically predicated our relationship on a mutual love of beer and its effects. Toward the end of the ride I passed him up, drinking vodka around the clock. I kept saying "I know I'm drinking too much and I'm gonna stop but not yet." He'd find my vodka bottles under the bed (very creative, eh?), be concerned, and then help drink up the bottle. Pretty entangled behavior.

He went with me to my second AA meeting and introduced us both as "probably being alcoholics." Since then he's revised his opinion and feels uncertain about whether or not he has a problem. When I first quit, I thought I had to feel that his drinking was none my business and that wanting him to stop his more "controlled" drinking was just a control issue. After a couple of weeks, I realized I couldn't handle any alcohol in the house and REALLY hated it when I could tell he had been drinking. Right or wrong, it was/is how I felt/feel.

The thing that surprised me was that he really seemed to feel my drinking was a problem (which it was) but didn't seem frightened enough of it to willingly eliminate it from his life, if only just to be supportive.

As you probably know, when one person quits it sends out shock waves that reverberate through pretty much every level of your relationship. We're sorting through the rubble now, seeing what's left, what we have in common, etc. The first few months were really rocky.

He no longer drinks around me but when he or I go out of town he does. I can always tell if he's had even 2 because he articulates everything very carefully. I wish I couldn't tell or wouldn't mind, but I do because it feels disloyal. Especially since he has 1st hand knowledge of how it was and knows how much is at stake.

Sometimes I fear our marriage may not survive my sobriety. Only time will tell. But I DO know I'd rather be sober and single than drunk and married. I'm looking forward to reading what others have to say about this and how they've handled this sort of thing. I've been wondering about that quite a bit. I still feel somewhat uncertain of what I have a right to ask for.

4/15/99

A Long Convoluted Story

By Bonnie L.

I have been sober for almost 6 months. My SO drinks and uses. Our relationship has always been affected by drugs and alcohol. We met in a bar. For the first 10 years I don't think we ever had sex sober! It defined our social activities, our circle of friends, how we communicated to each other and how we resolved (or attempted to resolve) our interpersonal problems and relationship/family issues. Alcohol was either the basis of our problems or how we dealt with a problem. We have been together for 16 years.

I started getting sober about 5 years ago. I now have almost 6 months. What I have discovered these past 5 years as I went through many relapses was how much my drinking patterns influenced his drinking/using patterns. We tried to outdo each other it seemed. But, when I'm not drinking, his drinking diminishes so much, I wonder if he even has a problem sometimes (I know he does though).

The first time I quit — I did so for 2 years via AA. I was convinced (thanks to my sponsor and other supportive (?) people in AA that if K. didn't also quit our relationship was doomed. I was told that I needed to go to Al-Anon as well as AA (yikes!!). I agonized over it, I pleaded with him to come to AA, I threatened him that I would have to leave — all the time crying inside because he is my best friend, and I didn't want him out of my life.

This time around, my sobriety feels different. I don't want to dictate to anyone else how they should handle their addiction/problems nor do I want to lay down expectations around when/if alcohol will be allowed in the house. Now, having said that, it's a struggle — Hell, I'm no saint, I get really annoyed if he has been drinking and absolutely intolerant if he can't carry on a conversation with me. But I quit ranting and raving (well, most of the time) about it and now I simply tell him he can't talk properly nor is he making sense and walk away. That has more influence on him than any of my previous pleading, threats, etc.

So, in many ways, it is easier this time around. Because I have changed -- not him. My attitude has changed.

I sincerely hope that K. will also quit and, I kinda think he will, but not because of any rule or threat from me. Anyway, that's my long, convoluted story about drinking and relationships. Now it is time to get out into that beautiful sunshine — what a glorious spring day it is!!

4/17/99

The Night of the Living Dead

By Jeff J.

I went to an AA meeting last night and was thoroughly bored to death. I sat and let my eye wander around the room and this is what I saw. I saw two older men dressed like youngsters, one who had to be pushing 60 but had an earring and was wearing flip flop shoes. I guess he thought he was looking real beachy. They both caught my eye because they were not paying attention to the meeting either; then I noticed that they both had real bad rugs on. Poor things were out trying to get some I guess. I saw three other people nodding off, and I saw a lesbian couple who were making eyes at each other. Most of the people just were sitting there with blank looks on their faces smoking one cigarette after another and sipping coffee. I tried real hard to understand and identify with what the topic was but I really couldn't tell you what the topic was.

About half way through the meeting I noticed a friend who was just as bored as I was and it occurred to me that this meeting was like the night of the living dead. Whatever it was they were talking about didn't have anything to do with anything real. It was one of those meetings were the leader chooses his buds to expound on a topic so vague that they end up rambling on about nothing. I would have liked to raise my hand and tell them that I hadn't had a thought to drink in a while but after attending that meeting, oblivion seemed like a viable option. But instead I sat like everybody else and waited, waited until the end so I could talk about what was really going on with me with a real friend that knew me.

It occurred to me that those meetings were nothing more than a medium for egomaniacs to postulate their interpretation of "the program" in front of other egomaniacs who sit and prepare their speech in silence. It is very sick.

Suddenly I realized what an AA meeting or an SOS meeting or any other "meeting" was for. YOU GO TO SOBRIETY MEETINGS TO MEET SOBER PEOPLE. Wow what a concept. So if you go to a meeting and sit in the back row and smoke ten cigarettes and think about what you're going to have for dinner after the meeting, you've missed the whole point and purpose of the meeting. I believe that a vital part of my sobriety is the people I meet at the meetings and who become good friends. I can't stay sober in this drunken world without sober friends. I have tried. I need other people with the same problem to talk to and to share my most intimate thoughts with. So from now on I am going to make it a point to really meet people at my meetings -- AA, or SOS -- and not just sit like everybody else and stare.

4/17/99

Spirituality: The Less Said the Better

By Peter V.

During my time in AA, I was forced to contemplate my spirituality -- something I'd never done before. As I've drifted away from that formal program, I continue to develop my own spirituality and believe that -- for me -- the connection to something bigger than myself is a crucial element of my sobriety. Spirituality is not the only thing that keeps me sober, but I'd never deny its importance for me.

The problem comes when there are large groups of people (as in AA) trying to talk about their spirituality. This talk often involves comparisons and one-upmanship.

I find that in order not to cheapen my own spirituality, it's best not to talk about it. It's an inherently personal and subjective thing, and the less said to others (in most cases), the better.

My own sense of the spiritual becomes mundane and is in some important way corrupted by public discourse. Further, when people try to talk about the spiritual with one another, it starts resembling one of those AA meetings like the one described below. Nobody knows what the speaker is talking about.

I thought that this strategy might be helpful to others.

April 18, 1999

Onionism: the Disease

By MOG

It is interesting, I have found, that my eyes don't tear as much when I don't chop onions. Some might say that I have a not so rare disease that is always there and manifests itself when the onions appear on the cutting board. Perhaps. If I stay away from the onions, it doesn't seem to matter whether I have onionism.

April 24, 1999

Powerless Is Not a Healthy Feeling

By Betts

Hello, All -- I just got a distress call from a friend in AA some of you might be able to identify with. She's a single mother, kids about 4 and 7, their father still using. It's a foggy, drizzly Sunday out here. Both kids are at home with her, doing their 'she did...', 'he did...' kid stuff. Her father's back in the hospital. Her mother's still drinking too much. She's going bananas.

Her sponsor told her to write down all the things she felt powerless over. I listened to her for a while, she getting downer and downer as she went on. Finally said, in my genteel, grandmotherly way: "That's bullshit, baby -- You know what you can't do anything about. Try concentrating on what you can do. Bundle them up and take them for a walk. Make some soup. Put away the dishes. Play a game with them in front of the fireplace. Then you won't feel quite so powerless. It is not a healthy feeling right now."

So now I'm waiting for a bolt of lightning to strike me. Sorry, folks — just had to blow my top. Back to my own chores. Peace!

April 25, 1999

Response, by Carol L.

Your friend is so fortunate to have you to turn to! This last round with AA my sponsor told me something similar when I was feeling trapped in a very abusive job. Since one of the reasons I have drunk in the past was to gain any sense of power over my life, it was THE worst exercise in the world. I have never understood the concept of how feeling powerless would help anyone stay sober. You gave great advice!

April 26, 1999

There Is No In-Between For Me

By Lisa P.

I have been thinking about my recent problems. I figure that I can either "practice alcoholism" or "practice sobriety." That's really how I feel about it. Both are actually a technique for coping. And I can make the choice, one way or the other. However, all I have to do is consider the option of do I want to make important decisions while: 1) I am drunk, or 2) I am sober — the choice becomes easy. The fact that I choose to "practice sobriety" all the time is really my business. And making that choice makes me feel empowered.

Have I figured out exactly what I am going to do yet? Nope. But will I do it sober? Yup.

Think about it -- do you want to drive a car 1) drunk, or 2) sober? Have conversations with your kids, significant other while you are 1) drunk, or 2) sober? In light of our friend Bill's situation, care for an ailing loved one while 1) drunk, or 2) sober? Live life: 1) drunk, or 2) sober?

Seems so basic, but I always try to look at things in that light, because there is no "in-between" for me. I am either drunk or I am sober. Yes, I was always sober at work, but I lived the life of a drunk. However now, life sober has been far, far better — maybe some rough moments, but in a word, better. And, SO much easier — and since I am basically lazy, "easy" is a good thing!

Thanks all — feels good "saying" it out loud — Lisa

April 23, 1999

Exulting in That Feeling

By Kate M.

> *Liz wrote: I have just read two emails in a row that mentioned the exhilaration of the early days of not drinking. That's where I am now, and am very disappointed that it will wear off. Kind of like a new love, I guess.... The exhilaration is what's keeping me in there fighting right now.*

Actually a lot of it's come back now. It never wore off as such, I just forgot what it was that was producing it every day at first. It didn't come from nowhere, that feeling -- it wasn't random. It was there every day at the start because I had clearly in my mind the difference between my daily life as a nondrinker and my daily life as a drinker -- I couldn't forget that, it was at the front of my mind back then.

I guess I've just let thinking about the difference slide, and taken it all for granted a bit ... as I said in my second mail, investing a bit of time in actively remembering why I stopped and the many downsides of drinking have made a world of difference. I've caught myself once again walking round my flat thinking "Isn't this great!! I'm walking round feeling totally well and clearheaded and sober!!" and exulting in that feeling.

It's important for me to remember what produces that feeling of exhilaration. I find right now that every word I wrote down about how I felt ten or eleven months ago when I stopped is invaluable in reminding me of things that have got a bit vague and blurred with time, even though a bit of hard thinking also brings them back.

April 26, 1999

My Sobriety is a Treasure

By Lisa P.

Well, who said the exhilaration was going to wear off? I still get a particular thrill out of being sober. I heard something about "rose colored glasses" and similar nonsense at AA meetings. When it didn't wear off for me, people in my aftercare class did their standard -- told me I was in denial. Sad, silly people. I believe some people spend too much time wallowing in their despair at giving up alcohol to take advantage of having a new outlook & lease on life.

I am driven forward by the changes I notice. This is what keeps me going, and promotes the continued "exhilaration." Small things, but I notice. And I take the time to notice. Like my skin looks so much better. My hands don't shake. I actually have friends and even better, can make plans with them and actually show up! Looking for these changes is like watching your hair grow -- it is so slight and infinitesimal, that you could stare in the mirror all day and see nothing. But as time racks up, you can look back and see all of the encouraging changes to your life.

I crave the very "ordinariness" of life now. Not having the additional woes created by myself after a day-turns-into-night of drinking. Having things run "somewhat" smoothly, or at least more smoothly then they ever, ever did when I was drinking. I have learned that life is actually "easier" sober.

It's the little stuff that still, to this day, impresses me. I buy cheap cut flowers from the street vendor every Friday (money saved from not drinking -- wait until you see how this adds up if you want a little exhilaration!) and take them home. It makes me happy. And reminds me how much a treasure my sobriety is.

April 27, 1999

Eating the Prey Alive

By Pippa M.

This evening my husband and I came home from 3 days in the north of the country on a game farm. It was a strange thing, being there, not 100 km from where I spent most of my childhood, riding through the Kalahari bush that I had not seen in nearly 30 years, all the almost forgotten birds and the animals.

Some weeks before I left I had been feeling very despondent about my capacity to beat this addiction thing. In the drive from Johannesburg airport to the northwestern border of the country, so many memories came flooding back. Riding past my now dead brother's old property. Seeing all the acacias, all the grass. All of it was almost too painful to bear. I decided that I would never make this struggle, it was going to defeat me for sure, I do not have it in me.

We spent many hours in the early morning and evenings, riding around in an open Land Rover with a game ranger. Many times I thought how nice it would be for you all to see real Africa this way. So many animals for whom life is just the now. No searching for some greater meaning, more understanding, more sanity. Just the now. Where living and dying has nothing to do with choice. Where each creature has its place in the food chain. One morning we came across a pack of seven wild dogs. These one doesn't often see. They were on a hunt, circling, scheming, trying to find a young buck or other prey. We followed them some three hours, until we lost them. I wasn't sad we hadn't seen them find their meal, since they often start eating the animal before they have even killed it. It is so hard to face how cruel nature really is.

But there were many other things also. A huge herd of elephant, and us being mock charged by the matriarch. A mum black rhino not ten metres away, her young calf suckling. Giraffe, impala, springbuck, kudo, gemsbuck, eland, wildebeest, a civet. Saw no big cats though. Warthogs romping in the water hole just outside our cabin. A bateleur eagle with its vivid plumage. Many many birds.

None of this is going to help any of you with your addictions, but it might help me. Reclaiming the past, perhaps, and laying it properly to rest. I didn't even smoke the weekend, and when the peach brandy came out, which is lethal stuff and right up my addiction alley (a bit like tequila) I wasn't even tempted to smell it.

So I survived for now. I don't think my train of thought makes a whole lot of sense tonight, and I hope you'll forgive the irrelevant content.

Thanks for being in it together.

May 9, 1999

Recovery Is a Process

By Ron C.

The state of recovery isn't an end state of not using ... it is a process of sobriety, relapse, success, failure, joy and pain ... and a lot of work

If we could all realize that we are addicts and that not using was the answer ... and could do that ... this list and recovery programs wouldn't exist.

When I realized that I was alcoholic and must become abstinent ... that was the beginning of my discovery of why I used, when I used, what kept me from stopping before and what was preventing me from maintaining sobriety now.

The denial part is: if you don't see recovery as a process ... you are in denial of the difficulty and work that is required ... you will self blame and other blame rather than slipping and then immediately getting back to the work of figuring out how the hell that happened so that it won't happen that way again.

May 19, 1999

Focusing On Sobriety

By Steve B.

There has been a lot said here lately about sobriety and relapse. A lot of this takes the form of confessions, explanations, and remedies. The remedies I am reading here seem to involve pharmacology, psychology, or the distraction of keeping busy in one way or another.

At the present time, I haven't had a drink for 13 days, and it has been easier than I had expected, so far that is.

I have been reading the posts every day, contributing occasionally, sometimes gathering a few pearls of wisdom from others, sometimes forming some conclusions of my own distilled from what I read as well as from my own experience. I would like to share a few of these.

Sobriety does have a certain momentum once it is set in motion, like a car moving down the road. However, it needs an engine to keep it moving, or it will come to a stop. I reach this conclusion from my experience of relapsing after six months of sobriety that I had initially set in motion through going to AA meetings. When I stopped attending meetings, my determination to stay sober began to weaken.

The support and sharing of thoughts and feelings among alcoholics is the true strength of any recovery group, whatever its ideology or absence thereof. This thought comes from my own experience as well as my noticing of people in this group speaking of needing to go to an AA meeting although they disagree with the most fundamental beliefs of AA.

Whatever we pay attention to grows. Focusing on sobriety, spending time thinking about it, writing about it, and reading about it places an investment in sobriety that makes us less and less inclined to give it up. Focusing on the shame, self-hatred, or helplessness we may feel as a result of relapsing only serves to increase these feelings and does nothing whatever to enhance sobriety itself.

The matter of staying sober is a lifetime commitment, something I will probably never be able to set aside and forget about.

May 19, 1999

My First Year's Fine Journey

By Ken M.

To all the new people on the list welcome -- this is a good place with some fine support available when needed. *Wilkommen till alla nya folk fran Norden som ar pa den har fin Nykterhets listan.*

Well it has now been one year today since I last partook in the consumption of Alcohol. And a fine journey on this new road it has so far been. It took 28 years of drinking, some drugging, a bunch of half-hearted attempts at quitting (none lasting better than 30 days) and a whole lot of agony to finally get it. I do not want to drink. It benefits me not a whit. Whatever I got from the high, the buzz, the relief -- it always cost a whole lot more than I finally was willing to pay. It took that final month of bingeing one pint (vodka) + 1/2 rack (beer) on a nearly daily basis to realize that it was

1. Putting my relationship with my family at risk
2. Putting my job at risk
3. Putting my health at risk
4. Impinging on family finances
5. Killing friendships right and left
6. Endangering myself and anyone within striking distance of my vehicle
7. Taking a real gamble with my continued liberty.

I also have a different take on the 7th line as then I felt that it had already removed my liberty by imprisoning me in my alcoholic behavior. Like the AA heads say -- I got sick and tired of feeling sick and tired.

With pressure from my wife I called the treatment center that my employer health insurance would cover and made an appointment for an assessment. Gee, guess what? The counselor felt I qualified as an alcoholic. Duh? As I was voluntarily placing myself in a treatment program I had no doubt. Why would he?

Almost walked out of there though. He described the treatment plan and said I would have to go to three AA meetings a week. Nope, not appropriate. Tried that a couple of years before and found I would drink more than prior to going.

I asked if there was something other than AA as it was not for me (I actually was quite adamant about this) and if that was the only choice I was out of there. He then reached into his file drawer and (reluctantly) gave me a four year old RR list of about six meetings in the Seattle area. He said I don't know too much about this group, I have sent clients to them in the past but then would soon stop seeing them (this was a problem?).

Started going to the treatment meetings and found a number on the list that was still valid. Went to what I understood to be a Friday RR meeting and found that they were shifting away from Trimpey's RR and looking for a different philosophical base. Treatment was a blend of 12-step, some Gorski relapse prevention and a touch of modified RET (the counselors' version cause he has a certificate in counseling from a local Community College). The support meetings were drifting to SMART recovery, which made sense, as the SMART recovery organization was founded by ex-RR board members.

From that meeting found others involved in non-12 step recovery and got a list of a few websites I might find of interest. While in smartrecovery.org found the link to unhooked.com and started reading.

Like those in Casablanca who had to wait and wait and wait, I read and read and read. Here I was most impressed by the Keepers and making a Personal Toolbox for Sobriety. The Sobriety Priority (I will not take a drink no matter what) dovetailed nicely with Rational Recovery's Big Plan (I will not take a drink ever again). Using AVRT I was able to get past the panic of the little bastard on my shoulder (the 'beast') saying I (it) will die without drinking. Just a beer would taste real good right now. Come on a couple of slugs of vodka -- no one will know. Well I would know, the aftertaste would be terrible (smells bad too), and no I (though it might) would not die without alcohol.

About 30 days into this the cravings were beginning to diminish in frequency and intensity. Something else started to rear its ugly head. An understanding that liking the 'buzz' was not the only reason I drank. Emotional repression is a big, big deal for me. Swift flashes of anger would also crop up as an issue that had to be dealt with. I found that working REBT's ABCs is an effective way for working through some of these other problems that are also at root to my addiction.

Whether alcoholism should be defined as a disease (along with drug addiction) is cause for endless debate at SMART Recovery meetings. I have no problem with this as the unifying point is that it can be arrested by modifying one's behavior. Found the Saturday Seattle SOS meeting but alas was only able to attend once as Saturday is the busiest day in my business and I must work. I manage a Tire and Auto Service Center for that big rubber company with blimps.

A bit of history -- the first AA meeting, where Bill W. met Dr. Bob was at the Sieberling estate in Akron, Ohio. Sieberling was the founder of Goodyear. I love useless coincidences -- but I digress.

A few weeks into sobriety I took the plunge into my first e-mail list. This was here; now called sosmail@onelist.com. It's been great. Marty, MOG, Rex, Lin, everybody, I can't thank you enough for all of your help. BTW I miss Rex -- probably a lot of us do. I don't always agree -- but that would be boring. I like the slight undercurrent of near anarchy -- this is not boring. I do appreciate the general civility of this group, but can handle the slings and arrows when let fly.

Time passed and some clarity kicked in at about 90 days sober. Finished the treatment program at 5 months. Another sense of well-being kicked in at six months. Not to say that all becomes sweetness and light. Many many problems and issues to deal with still -- don't some people call that life?

I created a new non-12 Step Recovery Support Group list for the Puget Sound area which is updated and (re)distributed to hotlines and treatment centers as necessary. This one is done as a tri-fold so it makes a nice handout. If anyone is interested I would be happy to mail out copies if you send me a postal address. I tried to convert it to be e-mailable -- didn't work -- so much to learn so little time. I also have been involved with getting the local SMART meeting facilitators to have separate monthly meetings for mutual support, better communication and improved credibility. While the little bastard on my shoulder still pipes up (albeit rarely) the various tools of support I use:

Unhooked.com website
SOSmail@onelist.com
SMART meetings
My family
My cats
Keepers
Sobriety Priority
AVRT and Big Plan
Running a small meeting list
Shifting Thinking
Focus on Consequences
REBT

provide a fairly solid positive foundation for staying sober. And one more -- I found out I have Hepatitis C -- while I have no symptoms from it (though interferon/ribaviran is a real bitch) alcohol is one fuel I will no longer add to that Dragon's fire. Thank You again for all your support and help -- I hope I can give back just a little of what I have received. You were warned this was long.

Pacem.

May 26, 1999

My Old Pattern

By Steve B.

It's certainly not my place to predict what will happen when someone else takes a drink after a period of abstinence, but I can relate my own experience.

When I was nearing the end of a sober period, the recurring thought that perhaps I was not really an alcoholic at all would come to mind more and more frequently. Eventually, I would convince myself that I could take just one or two drinks this time and I would try it.

Usually, the experiment seemed to vindicate my thoughts. I would have a drink and not touch another for several days. But the thought of drinking would not leave my mind. Although I seemed to be managing alcohol just fine, I was always thinking about when I would allow myself to drink again, and I would "reward" myself for being such a good moderate drinker by taking another drink.

This sort of thinking has always got me back into my old pattern after a period of from a week to a month.

I don't know whether my taking a drink at a ceremonial occasion would cause me to lose my sobriety or not, but I wouldn't want to try it. The loss of sobriety has cost me too much for me to want to risk it.

June 7, 1999

What Matters Is What I Do About It

By Carl W.

I find feelings of "shame, self-hatred, or helplessness" to be distinctly unproductive when it comes to getting sober. I was riddled with them at first. Even more damaging was my fury at all I had lost professionally, financially, and otherwise from my alcoholism. I really beat myself over that. These feelings made it difficult to stay sober. My customary way of dealing with such emotions for years had been alcohol. It was hard to learn completely new behavior to escape the cycle of regrets and drinking.

I read a lot about alcoholism. I discovered just what an intractable problem alcoholism is. Alcoholism is the despair not only of those victimized by it but also those who spend their careers trying to help us. If you think it's tough being alcoholic, consider the plight of the therapist/counselor. Most alcoholics never make a sincere effort to get sober no matter what. Of those who do go into a therapeutic program, most numbers I could find show that about two thirds relapse within sixty days. Very few are sober at the end of a year and at two years. Something is wrong with how we treat alcoholism (I happen to think that the bureaucracies' heavy commitment to AA and rejection of scientific approaches is a large part of the problem).

I don't have many feelings of shame, guilt, or regret nowadays. I consciously tried to get over that. This was not easy, since I was reared in an extremely fundamentalist Protestant home where every question, especially something like alcoholism, had a moral dimension. But I rejected that ridiculous religion and the notions of guilt and morality associated with alcoholism and it helped me immensely.

My present attitude toward why I am alcoholic is kind of a muddle, but I think it's a kind of helpful muddle. Most therapists I think would agree with it. I don't buy the disease model of alcoholism. What I do believe is that I have an inbred predisposition towards alcoholism. I didn't have my first drink until I was 21 in the Navy. I instantly loved it and was drinking alcoholically almost immediately. That tells me something. I didn't have a clue about alcoholism and didn't consider myself one for several years. It wasn't discussed as much in those years as it is today. I happened to read a column in The New York Times one day on alcoholism. It had one of those little checklists to help you determine if you're an alcoholic. I aced it, which rather distressed me. I knew then what I was dealing with or at least what its name was. I didn't try to get help until a few years later, however. I just felt terrible about being a drunken alcoholic.

I finally wound up in AA, which was a big relief for awhile. At least somebody understood what a struggle I was going through. I bought it hook, line, and sinker, or at least made a strong effort to do so, because I was desperate. I objected to religion and the messy logic of AA, but I suspended my usual skepticism because I was desperate and the way I was living was only causing my life to deteriorate markedly.

I have finally pieced together a group of attitudes toward alcoholism that work for me. It took me a long time to get where I am now, but I have stronger sobriety than I ever have. My present attitudes are based directly in my own experience and draw from my reading and observations of others. I don't feel guilty about any of my drinking. (This was a long time coming.) The bitterness over what I have lost because of my drinking has been the most difficult part. But I have been able to get over even most of that. I don't feel responsible for being alcoholic. It's just something I was saddled with when I was born. Whether that is a gene or whatever doesn't matter to me. Because of a particular confluence of heredity, family, culture, etc., I became an active alcoholic. What matters is what I do about it. The regrets over my losses I have come to accept as having been predetermined as well.

Life is notoriously unfair. What we get from life is largely determined by sheer luck. It has far less to do with our conscious efforts than we like to think. Even the capacity to work hard to be a "success" in life is largely determined by genetic and social factors over which we had little or no control. I have known a good many extremely wealthy people in my life. Some of them are very nice, interesting people. But I can't think of a one who "deserved" what they had.

It was all largely accidental, and the ones among them who have any sense will tell you as much. I just happen to have been given the opposite end of the spectrum when it comes to what life can offer.

A counselor told me just a month ago when I was going over my history that my life had been a string of horrors. The mere fact I was still alive through all of it surprised her. She kept probing about suicide. Finally, I asked her, "You think I'm vulnerable to suicide, don't you?" She paused and said, "Yes, I do. You have strong indicators that place you in the highest risk group. I am interested to see how you've escaped it." I knew exactly what she was talking about, but suicide has not been particularly a problem for me.

I think my attitudes toward the unfairness and happenstance of life has a lot to do with my ability to keep going even though things appear very bleak. Looking at life in terms of good and evil, just and unjust, is an immature attitude borrowed from Christian religions who manipulate through guilt and forgiveness. It is simply an incorrect, nonproductive world view ... unless you're the pope or Pat Robertson or Jerry Falwell or head up a drug enforcement task force and have a vested interest in continuing the delusion.

Relapse has been a huge problem for me. I think it is for most alcoholics and I also think most people who do it don't talk about it. It's far more pervasive than even the dismal data show. My attitude toward relapse now is that it is a part of trying to get sober. Even if you don't actually relapse, you are deliberately dealing with the possibility of relapse to stay sober. The key is to get back on track on immediately. Gradually your periods of sobriety will get longer and it will get easier. You also must work not to just accept relapse by saying, "Well, it's just part of it and I couldn't help myself." Somehow you've got to get to be able not to beat yourself up over a relapse but not to get comfortable with relapsing either. If you accept relapses easily, before long their duration will increase and you'll find yourself back in full blown drinking, quite likely just as bad as when you first tried to quit or even worse.

Study your relapses. What are you going through when

they occur? For different people, it's different things. For me, almost all relapses occurred when I had money, time, and was determined to have a sexual adventure. Once set in motion, the relapse caused a return to my old cycle of drinking every few days or once a month or so. For some people, they relapse when they undergo some sort of reversal ... never a triggering factor for me. For others it's the attitude of their mate. What it really is, is one's alcoholic tendencies trying to find a way to express themselves. It has little to do with actual circumstances.

I charted my relapses for a while. I was amazed to see that there was a cycle of about 45 days for relapsing for a long while. It had not much to do with what was actually happening in my life. It was as though there was some sort of built in clock determining when I would relapse. That knowledge proved very useful. Our attitudes often don't bear a close relationship with what is actually happening (ever laugh at a funeral?). They are biologically determined. That does not mean they aren't subject to conscious management if we are aware of them.

Dealing with alcoholism becomes a process of looking at life in purely mechanistic terms for me. I call it the "monkey wrench philosophy of life." My life is like an old car. It calls for constant maintenance, creativity in finding missing parts, and prolonged commitment. But keeping up an old car is not only ecologically responsible and very cost effective, it's an exercise in discipline and gets to be kind of fun. It marks one as counter-cultural. I love being that. If I manage my old car properly and keep it up, anticipating what it needs, not just reacting to breakdowns, over time I will end up with a unique, attractive car, something to be genuinely proud of.

I recently acquired my grandmother's old 68 Chevy Impala. I can't wait to restore it. Every day someone stops to relieve me of the piece of junk in my driveway. I don't tell them I know exactly what I've got. I just tell all rednecks who stop, "Oh I dunno, I'll hafta thank about it and get back to ya. Ya see that was my mama's and my grandma's car and I wouldn't feel right a-selling it." They hate me. I love it.

May 19, 1999

Glad for the Second Chance

By Dee K.

I've been watching my 18 month old son wander around naked, except for one of my sandals and some mardi gras beads. He has a piece of star-shaped cat food stuck to his forehead (from experimenting with eating just like the kitty), and is trying, most earnestly, to hold onto his penis while he walks. That's no small feat, given how far his tummy sticks out, and how small the object of his affection is!

I was thinking how I would have missed all the simple beauty and hilarity of this moment if I were drunk, getting drunk, or hung over. Now, to watch this brings tears and laughter all at once. I am so profoundly glad to have a second chance to live this life, with all its concomitant joy and sorrow. At this moment it feels so simple and utterly worthwhile to be here for all of it.

I just needed to share this joy with some people who know how precious our sober realities are. Thanks for listening.

June 7, 1999

The Fuckit Switch

By Lin L.

C.W. posted: My last relatively lengthy abstinence ended while I was standing in Rite-Aid. Suddenly, I happened to notice the beer display and The Cloud descended over my head. "Why not?" "Who cares?" "What difference does it make?" These were my thoughts.

Ah, the infamous "fuckit switch." As in, "Aw, fuckit, I'll just have one." Or, "Ah, fuckit, I need a break." Or, "Ah, fuckit, I deserve a reward." In other words, any drinking-related thought that begins "fuckit" is probably not a good one.

The use of the word "fuck" in particular is important. That is a word that has a high emotional load -- grown men have been known to commit assault and sometimes even murder when they hear it. It effectively shuts down rational thought (thus the "tripped-circuit" result) and allows only strong emotions to pass through to consciousness. And, what do we do with strong emotions, boys and girls?

Also, the "fuckit" portion is usually only the first half of the equation. The second half is usually one of the many excuses we use to drink. "Ah, fuckit; I deserve this." "Ah, fuckit; I'll show those bastards." "Ah, fuckit, being sober never did me any good anyway." So, we disarm our ability to think reasonably in a goal-oriented way, and then the little devil on the shoulder moves in for the kill, with a totally irrational thought that we -- without the verbal land mine we just dropped on ourselves -- would be able to handle in a blink.

July 1, 1999

My Independence Day

By C.A. E.

Today was the "4th of July" (U.S. Independence Day) party at the American Consulate. I should have been but wasn't prepared for the barrage of alcohol. Waiters with trays of wine and beer stepped up to us as we entered the gates, and the smell was pervasive. I noticed one person with a glass of orange drink but, rather than hunt for it, opted for drinking nothing. That was O.K. because one of my primary reasons for being there was networking (at which I have to say I had some success).

Then I was invited to someone's house for "tea" with a group of women. I had to brace myself when I saw a huge bottle of champagne with glasses on the table. This was our tea?! I was fortunate, though, because three of the five of us didn't drink. In fact, the hostess got out a smaller bottle of champagne for the other two, and I indulged in a glass of cranberry juice.

I had a chance to use that glorious expression, "I can't drink." The hostess pushed a little, saying "Just for the toast," but I repeated, "I can't drink." She murmured something about Mormons (who are practically the only people in Japan who don't drink) and the others, even though they had barely met me, knew enough about me to have a good laugh. I was preparing some explanations in my head about osteoporosis and such, but no one even asked why I couldn't drink.

As each of the guests left the party at the Consulate, we were handed a "gift bag" containing an American orange (a nice treat since they're about $1.00 apiece here) and a can of Budweiser. Happy 4th of July!

I left my can with the hostess of our "tea party." I've never really liked beer, but I didn't even want the temptation of it sitting in my apartment.

Actually, I did much more than survive the "4th of July." I thoroughly enjoyed myself, and because of being sober will remember every minute of it. Hope other Americans on this list are able to have similar experiences.

Sober in Sapporo.

July 2, 1999

My Best Thinking

By Nick A.

I recently had a truly awful twelve step experience. The counselor who helped me get my now defunct SOS meeting started at the hospital has a string of halfway houses in the greater Tampa area. He does not run the organization as a "twelve step or hit the road program," but things can get very "steppy" around there anyway.... Last week there was a guest speaker who truly made my skin crawl.

His "story" had little to do with him. The only thing about him in the whole hour was that, at some point in time, he had moved to Tampa. He presented the "Fire and Brimstone" twelve step -- you're defective -- your best thinking got you here -- you're selfish and self centered -- pray to God -- there's NO other way -- half steps will avail you blah blah blah ... sermon. What really got me was the number of people in the room who sat and watched him with that thousand yard stare -- "where do I sign up for the get rich in real estate seminar" look in their eyes. They were awestruck by the majesty and brilliance of his presentation. All I can say is that my best thinking got me away from twelve step programs.

When I tried to explain my concept of the AA concept at my now defunct SOS meeting, it went something like this:

In 1936 when AA came into being they were trying to find what made alcoholics different than other people. They weren't taller, shorter, thinner, fatter, Black, White or any other thing that they could nail down. Genetics and chemical balances in the body were not well understood. Heck, penicillin was still years away!

What they could nail down seemed to be related to behavior. This behavior seemed to indicate that alcoholics were selfish and self centered, putting alcohol ahead of all else.

My belief has always been that these perceived character defects and self centered behavior were the result of alcoholism, not the cause. Once you are addicted to the stuff, of course it's your number one priority. Once you're an addict, without alcohol you can die from the withdrawal. Now with a dependency like that, where are you going to put your priorities?

July 5, 1999

Faced Another Demon

By Crystal D.

Just wanted you all to know that I've faced another demon. Went out of town today and visited the in-laws (hmmm ... guess I've faced two demons, huh?). The first one has been a recurring nightmare/daymare for me. Wondering how I'll do when faced with the aspect of having to be around a lot of drinkers and not be able to drink. For example, a bar or a social gathering. I've declined all party invitations up until now. But I've been putting off the in-laws for a year and a half and they were having no more excuses sooo ... off I went.

Well, I'm here to tell you, I've survived. On my way into Ohio, I had a layover in Cincinnati and I sat in a little bar there without even realizing where I was sitting. All I knew was that I wanted to smoke so my body sorta propelled me there. Anyway, I sat there and realized about ten or fifteen minutes into it, that I was in an actual bar. I couldn't believe it. I was sitting in a place filled to the gills with all the booze I could want (my pockets stuffed with cash) and I didn't have a drop. Lord knows I wanted one! I smoked two cigs and went on my merry way. Without as much as a glance back.

The last time I stopped drinking, I used to look at these places with longing. The television shows would make my mouth water. Now they aren't any different from any other place that I have no desire to go into i.e., sports stores or stores jammed with "guy stuff" (lol).

Demon number two was at the in-laws, around the pool. The cooler was passed and the beer was offered. I politely declined although my mother-in-law said that drinking wasn't bad as long as you only had "a few" (I'm not sure if those were her actual words but they were somewhere around that neighborhood), or a glass of wine never hurt anyone. I then told her, yeah that's good for some folks but I like it too much and although I know I should stop, my brain and the rest of me don't tend to agree all the time. We just sorta drink 'til we're full and then drink some more. We all had a big laugh out of that one. Mom is harmless and very supportive. I usually use the "I'm allergic to alcohol" line when I can and when there are "ignorant" folks around. However, I couldn't get away with it this time because it just so happens that the person whose house we were at is actually truly allergic to alcohol. There went my alibi. Also, she knows me. I couldn't weasel my way out of that one too easily. Thank goodness, too! I don't feel comfortable lying to the ones I love.

My husband however was very cautious throughout the whole ordeal. He asked me if it was ok for him to drink and if I was okay having it around. He then took a sip or maybe two and I didn't see him drink another drop the rest of the evening. Not that I was watching or anything. All that I can think now, is god how I love that man! This is also supposed to be my weekend to quit smoking. Yes, I'm jumping on that wagon again. I went to the store to get some patches and they wanted fifty bucks to start. Well, I'm still smoking. But that's another story. When we went to the store to get the patches, hubby says, "are we quitting smoking now too?" I said, I'm going to try and he said then I guess we're both quitting smoking together.

Isn't great to have someone in your corner no matter what? I'm glad he doesn't force me to do these things (it sucks to have someone tell ya what's good for ya!) and that I come to these conclusions on my own.

....still trying to quit the nic.

Your pal in sobriety

5 July 1999

Rough Encounters

By Abe C.

About the "Minnesota Method" -- I had a brush with these (for want of a better word) sadists about 6 months ago through an intervention instigated by my family.

Their efforts to break my will and their utter ruthlessness was something taken from the Spanish Inquisition with a dash of latter-day psychology.

Luckily for me I was not drinking at the time and maintained a measure of dignity. This enabled me to at least be aware of and understand their motivation.

After being made to feel that I was the worst creature that ever crawled out from under a rock and told that I would be dead in a matter of months if I did not book myself in as an inpatient, I really smelt a rat. Especially since I had a physical not long prior to this to find that my liver function and blood pressure were normal. In short, they were touting for business and really not interested in my well-being.

At least I had the satisfaction of telling the head of this institution what I thought of him and his methods at a face-to-face meeting a day or so later. He didn't take kindly to my suggestion to insert his wall mounted certificates "where the sun doesn't shine." LOL.

Needless to say, I did not admit myself and have managed to stay sober without a single relapse these past six months. All by my own volition.

It is small wonder that their recidivism rate is so high. How can a person, after being abused, made to work like a "housemaid", and continuously told that they are worthless because they abuse alcohol, not feel anger, bitterness and be totally demoralized? Especially after paying good hard earned money for this dubious healing process. It sure is a good set of triggers to start boozing again.

July 9, 1999

Comment by Joe B.:

I was asked to participate in this ritual once when my dad got hospitalized. I went along with it because I was told this was how they helped him realize the error of his ways and to shock him out of drinking anymore.

Hell, he was in for major liver damage as it was and anything said beyond that was just me getting the last word in on old wounds caused while growing up. He stayed on the program for awhile, then decided he couldn't handle the assholes in AA and stopped going. I saw him drunk once or twice after that and I was extremely upset that all my laser guided missiles at his flaws were all for naught.

We never had much of a relationship before or after this, and he has since barely survived a triple aneurism and is lucky to know who I am, but with everything I know now I am ashamed at the way we confronted him and can't see how any good could have come of it at that point.

Just my reflections.

July 10, 1999

Comment by Malina J.

Yesterday, I had a rough encounter with a psychiatrist who did not take kindly to my rejection of AA. She wanted to lock me in the looney bin on the spot. When I refused to permit myself to be hospitalized, she told me that I should be "medical boarded" out of the Army. Basically, get a disability stipend for being unfit for service due to mental illness. Then she told me that my anti-depressant medication clearly wasn't working, but decided not to change the medication I was on. After she was done terrorizing me, she sent me home. Now, was that the perfect set-up for a "relapse" or what???

If I thought that I was all alone in the world and the only person who felt the way I did, I would have been lost. Instead, I stuck to my beliefs and I refused to drink. I didn't anticipate such situations when I decided that "no matter what" was a good idea, but "no matter what" was a big, big help yesterday. Thank you all.

July 11, 1999

A Close Call

By Bill Mc D.

Howdy Everyone:

In an earlier post, Maggie used the word "Fragile" to describe her sobriety. How very true that turns out to be.

Before anyone panics or gets out the wet noodles or whatever, let me say that I did not slip, relapse, screw up, whatever you wanna call it. My sobriety is still intact, but it was a close fucking call. They have a saying, somewhere, that there comes a time when a sober alcoholic literally has no defense against the first drink. I was there today, and, boy, is it ugly....

I watched a horrific traffic accident happen today, on the way back from Petersburg, Virginia. It involved six cars/vans and an eighteen-wheeler. The truck flipped out of control, trying to avoid a van, and took several other cars with it. This blocked I-95 northbound completely for over three hours. At least one person, I was told by the Virginia State Police, died in this conflagration. The police were talking to me in the first place because I was in one of the first four cars immediately behind the accident. I saw the whole thing go down; it took maybe five seconds. And they -- the police -- wanted to know what I saw.

The clearest image I have of the whole thing is that of a dog, which I had to swerve to avoid, running away from the accident scene. He had been thrown clear from one of the vans involved and was unhurt; I have never seen terror like that in anything's eyes.

There was nothing to do, nowhere to go, and the temp was up at around 100, even hotter there on the pavement without the benefit of shade. So I answered a few questions and baked for three hours, all the while watching as hordes of paramedics, firemen, cops and tow-truck persons did their unenviable jobs. And I thought about how easily it could have been *my* van that got into the initial tangle with the rig; after all, I was only about a hundred yards behind the truck when it flipped. I was even closer when it started to go out of control and braking hard seemed suddenly like an excellent idea....

I don't want to go into a whole HALT thing again, but when they finally got traffic rolling again, I was in fact hungry and angry and very, very tired. And also very thirsty. The simple truth of the matter is this: If I had stopped to eat my belated lunch at a bar, I would have had a beer. Or two. Or ten. I don't know if I would -- or could -- have stopped the flow. I may very well have ended up in a seedy Holiday Inn room with a twelve pack and some take-out chicken. That is the truth. I was hot and tired and thirsty and pissed off and goddammit I wanted a damn drink.

Okay, so I stopped at a Burger King. Where I drank three full large cups of water while waiting for my grease burger, much to the amazement of the counter lady. And the thirst passed, but not the desire for beer. All the way home -- no Friday night out -- I kept thinking about how very little time it took for a lot of lives to go from normal to completely fucked. The whole gig -- sobriety, life, everything -- is a tightrope walk over Angel Falls, folks, and it don't take but a little breeze to screw everything up. And I finally arrived at the conclusion, two hours later, just outside Bethesda, where I know from the bars, that a drink was just the right kind of breeze, and the wrong kind of solution. What scares me is that it took me that long to get to that conclusion.

My house is very very clean now, and someplace in the midst of that whirlwind of housework, I just stopped cleaning and cried for about five minutes; I cried harder than I've cried for more months than I can count. I cried for me, for my Dad, for the people in the hospital and morgue as a result of that accident, for a lot of things and reasons and people. Most of all, I cried because something inside me snapped today, and that vicious little motherf*#^er on my shoulder was right there, dancing his little dance of joy and talking shit all over again. I played the radio loudly and sang along with everything to not hear him.

So, yeah, in the end, the tools I have always propounded worked, but I'm pretty damn glad that I don't have, say, cooking sherry or something around here. Because, all things considered, I guess I'm not that damn smart after all.

Pax, All. Peace.

July 9, 1999

I Was Brown and Sandy and Lively

By Brenda S.

I find that being drunk and fat is worse than being sober and fat. If you can quit drinking maybe you just might be able to get a grip on your health too.

Exercise is one of my best sobriety and body image tools. For me (a woman who hates sports and fears going fast down mountains) exercise means walking, dancing, swimming and stretching. Moving my body and breathing makes me feel more alive. Especially if I am outside. Also I have a better body image sober than drunk.

I was ashamed of being out of shape and felt helpless to change my body when I felt I could not stop drinking. Now we have something to be proud of. We do not drink. We can change.

So much energy goes into wishing we looked different etc. You are certainly not alone with your concerns over weight. Good for you for not jumping on those diet pills. Last January I went to a beach in Mexico all white and 15 pounds overweight, looking my age, 57. Not a pretty sight. After 3 days of walking on the beach and playing in the water and mellowing out, I saw myself in a much more accepting way. I wasn't fat and old anymore. I was brown and sandy and lively.

When you are gripped by sadness it is so hard to believe your feelings will change and your outlook will improve. Feelings always change, as GrandMog pointed out to me in a past post.

Hang in there and remember that, to us, you are always thin.

July 9, 1999

Stuff That Has Been Gone Awhile

By Sue G.

As one who drank for a lot of years, and damn near died from it, I can only speak for my own experience when it comes to living in the world. First of all, I have never participated in AA, only heard horror stories, and knew all about their powerlessness theories through clients (I am a social worker) who had been through the experience. Without going into all of the details, I rejected the thought of AA while still in the hospital recovering from my near-death experience (and I don't mean the light, either). My rationale was simple. I chose to drink. No one held a gun to my head. No one tied me up and stuck a funnel in my mouth. Therefore, I must take responsibility for this myself.

I have come to be very at peace with myself, most of the time. I once thought that it would be impossible to go from day to day without alcohol. I couldn't comprehend getting through an evening without drinking. And it sucked at first. In the first days home, the only thing that kept me from picking up a bottle of wine (and it was here, and still is) was the knowledge that I would die. Then I joined this list and my reasons became more day to day. I actually began to *like* waking up, going to work (gasp!) and spending my time sober. I found some stuff in myself that I had forgotten about. It had never gone away, it was just in there passed out (and NO, I didn't take a swim in Lake Me).

So there are a lot of things besides the physical that are great reasons for being sober. It just takes some time to recapture them, and relearn some of the stuff that has been gone for awhile.

July 14, 1999

Diverting a Stream

By Maggie R.

This whole process is a bit like diverting a stream -- at first you have to work very hard at forcing the water into the new channel, then you have to work very hard at keeping it flowing through the new channel, because it will take every possible opportunity to revert back to the old one, but over time the new channel gets deeper, and the stream flows through it naturally. Vigilance is still required, especially in times of danger, e.g. a flood, but in general you can rely on the stream to go the way you want it to go.

18 July 1999

Another Pair of Shoes

By Lisa P.

I will turn a year on Saturday. An entire life has evolved around me, and I would not give up for the world. When I first got sober, I presumed everything would be gray, that I would always be on edge without the beer to "calm me." I had no idea of the extent to which I was causing my own depression, literally. It took about 4 - 5 months for it to lift, but remarkably, it has. And it has stayed lifted. For this one fact alone, I cannot imagine going back.

But it goes so much further, really. I knew in order to stay sober, I would have to figure out another way to get through my problems. It has been "the answer" for so long. I knew if I didn't come up with something else, I would be right back where I started.

The booze was the shoes I wore, figuratively. If I took them off, and tried to walk over the terrain of life with "bare feet," I would step on rocks and cut myself -- I need to find another "pair of shoes." So out I went, to the big old internet, and began researching behavioral modification. I do not have time to go into it all now (not to mention it could get boring ...), but one of the best finds was Albert Ellis and Rational Emotive Behavior Modification. He is a well known psychiatrist and author, and I would recommend his basic primer of the same name above. Any book store carries it. He also has great stuff on anger and frustration. It's a matter of taking the time to practice thinking about things in a rational manner. It does mean one has to think before reacting to a situation.

Seems so obvious, now, but it took a while to get used to. I now strive to be proactive, not reactive.... I have many things going on in my life, some good, some bad.... Since being on this list, have learned to be more open minded. That has been one of the undeniable benefits of being a part of this. I know we don't meet face-to-face, but this is a form of interpersonal relationships. Watching out for each other, losing a friend from the list to alcohol from time to time, rejoicing in each others' victories, being an ear and a heart for someone's troubles — it all adds up.

20 July, 1999

Hand in the Flame

By Margo M.

I am amazed what damage was done by my Monday drinking. It took me until Thursday to begin feeling alright again (physically, mentally, and emotionally).

All these years of daily drinking had given me a sort of permanent hangover that I didn't recognize until I stopped drinking for a week last week. Physically, I was alert, energetic with increased stamina. Mentally, I was focused, able to concentrate and make decisions. Emotionally, I felt hopeful and happier than I'd felt in a long time. And this was just one week off alcohol!

But what I did on Monday really set me back. Just one day of drinking took me 3 days to recover. And I'm still not all the way back yet to the good place I was. I wrote about this in my Journal so I can go back and read it the next time I ask myself "Why not drink today?"

All in all, this relapse taught me a good lesson. On Monday, and for a couple of days following, I was back in that dark place where I felt isolated, scared, and depressed. Why in the world would I ever want to feel like that again? This is what I must remember.

Sometimes I believe that I am overthinking this whole thing. For instance, I know that I must not stick my hand into a flame. I don't go through the process of reasoning that "Yes, the flame is beautiful … I would like to touch it ... however, the extreme heat is bad for my delicate tissue … I would suffer a burn that would necessitate medical treatment … there may be permanent loss of function …" and on and on. No. I just know I cannot stick my hand into a flame. Period. I believe that I must relate to drinking the same way. JUST NO.

Margo

5 Aug. 1999

Rock and Roll Is Not Dead

By Sharon L.

I am happy to say I went to the concert and had a wonderful time. Stayed sober and everything. I was a little uncomfortable at first just because it was a new experience. My friends were wonderful, one only drinking cokes, and the other being very discreet about pouring rum into hers.

At first I felt like I was the only one sober, shrugged it off and bought a $2.50 bottle of water!! GASP. And started looking around -- yes there were lots of people drinking, but there were lots of people NOT drinking. I couldn't believe it. Gee, I never noticed before. After the water I was still feeling a little uneasy so I bought a $3.75 coke -- now we are talking -- I got more of what I paid for and it beat the $6 beer!!!

By the second band (there was 4) I was standing up, screaming and dancing (really more like standing in place, swaying), and laughing. All the feelings of "I am the only one ..." disappeared, I relaxed and the thought of drinking did not reappear. PLUS, I remember every long haired sexy good looking guy I saw!!! Totally amazing.

Then as the concert proceeded, I started watching the uncontrollable drunks showing up -- the guy a couple rows over that got escorted out by 3 security guards for being too rowdy, the 2 guys fighting over seats, the people that kept trying to get closer than allowed AND trying to smoke inside a no smoking arena. The whole thing became as amusing and entertaining as the concert itself. AND I was sober!!!!

Then as we were leaving the arena there was a woman passed out in the seat -- I mean totally passed out -- 4 guys were trying to get her up and she was limp as a rag doll -- I thought she was dead -- they couldn't get her up. Anyone that could sleep thru Ted Nugent was definitely out of it!! I have never done that but can only imagine how scary that can be, for her and her friends. BUT it wasn't me and it wasn't my friends -- I was sober -- it was both exhilarating and sort of surreal -- like that could have been me. For a moment -- I was sad -- what made me lucky enough to NOT be her -- and would she ever feel what I was feeling now -- leaving a concert, walking straight and tall, and proud of my accomplishment.

As we left and were walking back to our car I was still watching people, some staggering, some falling, wondering who was going to drive them home, and then realizing how many times I have done it. This time I could even walk up to the cop and ask him how to get back on the interstate -- with NO FEAR of being arrested. Even though he gave me bogus directions -- but that's another story.

Then we all went to eat, and laugh and talk and I remember and am not embarrassed about anything that I did. Life is good!!! Sorry for rambling but I had to share what I learned -- I can be sober, go places, have fun. Other people do it too (and I never noticed) and it FEELS wonderful!!! Thank you all for being here to listen to the good times as well as the bad. For anyone new starting out -- 10 months ago I would never have believed this was possible. I am living proof it is. ROCK AND ROLL IS NOT DEAD AND NEITHER AM I.

Still sober Sharon

7 Aug. 1999

A Dozen Years of Freedom

By Robert B.

Today I celebrate a dozen years of freedom from drinking. I chose from the start not to follow the path of the twelve steps, being a stubborn do-it-yourselfer and also having known enough about the dynamics of AA (the 'god' thing, if you will) and figured this was a personal matter between me and me.

It was not necessarily a "voluntary" thing from the start, having been given the ultimatum from my now ex-wife to a) get out of the house and b) quit drinking as conditions of my sentence to return in good graces.

I did both, and contrary to much anecdotal information to the contrary, it does sometimes take a kick in the ass (teeth, balls, or whatever may be applicable) to take that first leap to "I don't drink, no matter what."

The sobriety remains, the wife is different. When Natalie (my beautiful wife pictured with me on the photo gallery) and I first got married, it was understood that, if not a condition, at least we both knew that I could never drink again for me and this relationship. This was *not* a kick in the ass, but an acknowledgment that I was not, never was, and could never be a "normal" drinker, whatever in the hell that is. I am still amazed that someone can have *a* glass or two of wine with dinner, then not order any more. "Where the hell is the gallon?" the little red demon would ask.

I am sure that I have included this in my previous annual messages, but I will again. I was terrified in those first days and weeks that I could never have any fun again for the rest of my life if I didn't include alcohol as part of the fun. As the days, months, and now the years have gone by, this has been proven to be wrong over and over again. The fun of hugging the porcelain god in the middle of the night, weaving back and forth back home with a wing and a prayer (well, actually, maybe just a wish and not a prayer) hoping to get home in one piece, of endless, mindless arguments fueled by my copious consumption, ain't fun.

To you who have the same misgivings, that somehow you will miss something when you give up the drink, think of *those* grand things that you will miss. And the things you won't. You can still be funny. You can still go to parties. You can still dance, make love (probably better than ever), you can and will do the fun things in life which, in reality, become mutually exclusive of drinking.

I have often thought and commented on this list what, if anything, could possibly "force" me back into drinking again? Divorce, death of a loved one, finding out that I have a month to live? Nope. Nothing. It becomes a lifelong commitment, sometimes achieved a minute at a time, sometimes more, but a personal contract with yourself (and, of course, a little help from your friends) that there isn't anything that is going to force me to raise that glass to my lips. It's your choice, folks. Make it.

To all of you who celebrate a day, a month, a year and more of this sobriety which we all share (or are trying to), hearty congratulations. If you haven't found out yet, you will: It's worth it.

I look forward to a message a year from now posting #13, which will be a lucky number for me, just like the other 12. As Marty would say, "See you at the Secular Recovery Convention in September." I'll be there.

And, from the "365 Tao", this message to all:

"If the boulders are moved,
Even a river will change its flow."

21 July 1999

Holiday Survival Guide

By J.J. W., Carl W., C.A. E., Anne, Shirl, De W., Rex, Chris, Treena, Nancy, Jim Y., Marjorie, Brad, Ben B., Marty, Larry, Don, Bones, Bill M., Sue, Jennifer, MOG, Don G.

I hate the holidays.

I distrust the holidays.

I am at risk during the holidays.

So, I prepare for them in advance. Months in advance.

And there isn't a single holiday tradition that I am obligated to observe: I can ignore them, I can mock them, I can turn them upside down and create my own crazy but sober traditions.

J. J. W.

It is a commonplace in discussions of alcoholism that alcoholics are especially vulnerable during holidays. This is probably so (suicides spiral around Christmas, for example) but it needn't be the case.

Why are holidays such a big deal for alcoholics? They tend to point up to the alcoholic the shortfalls in his life (which everybody has, but particularly alcoholics). The image that somehow life has failed the alcoholic is used by the alcoholic as a reason to drink, as if he really needed one. This image is reinforced by advertising, and never underestimate the power of advertisers. If you aren't out consuming, you're not with it. Most retail sales are made around Christmas, of course, which has reached obscene proportions. I fully expect Christmas trees to start appearing in malls about the 4th of July before much longer.

I used to buy into much of this. During the worst of my drinking before I knew what was going on with me, I was terribly depressed around New Year's, Christmas, and the like. I never got invited to the kind of parties I wanted to go to (I thought everybody else did, however.) So I started giving my own. They were wildly extravagant and totally nuts and very, very popular. A lot of booze, of course. I quickly found that that sort of entertaining didn't accomplish a thing but increase my bills enormously. When the party was over, I seldom got invited to anything anywhere nearly comparable to what I had done. The A List people, a fickle and self-centered crowd, moved on to the next party, and there I sat. I was a total fool.

Then I went into AA. I was almost totally isolated by then with no friends thanks to alcohol. When the holidays came around no invitations. So I decided I would just celebrate them by myself. Which I did. I would make myself a wonderful dinner and then go to a play or concert (I was amazed to learn that a lot of very nice people do things like that on holidays) and go to bed early. After I did it a time or two, I found I really enjoyed spending holidays that way. No hangovers. No huge bills. I would see people on New Year's Day still straggling home, and I felt fine, clear-eyed, and energetic and admittedly a little holier than thou.

I was doing all this in Manhattan. In reading New York City history, I discovered that New Year's Day used to be the biggest holiday of the year in the city, not New Year's Eve or Christmas. It was a custom surviving from the Dutch and New Amsterdam apparently. Until well into the twentieth century, Manhattanites would have an open house on New Year's Day and send invitations to people that they would be "at home" that day. People would travel from house to house visiting where they would be served lovely food and drink. Young men would travel in groups and use one another's invitations to get in. Girls loved all this, of course, because they got to meet a lot of new men. There was much drinking, of course, among certain sets, but it was a very elegant custom. One could tell where one stood socially by the sort of open houses one went to. It was a preferred way to meet new people when calling cards and introductions were the order of the day.

So for the few years I was still in New York, I started having an open house on New Year's Day. I would have beautiful food and flowers. I kept the guest list fairly small and there was no booze. If people didn't know I was alcoholic, I just told them I knew they might appreciate the opportunity not to drink any more booze and served three kinds of excellent coffee, juices, and a punch in a cut glass bowl I got from my grandmother. Even the drinkers liked to be treated with such civility, I found. I tried to avoid inviting anybody who might be abusing alcohol, but if one did show up, they sobered up.

Since there was no alcohol and the group was small, people could actually talk and get to know one another, which was the whole point. These non-alcoholic parties turned out to be far more successful than the sodden extravagances I had formerly gone for. And people invited me to dinner and I actually made friends. It was astounding!

Now I don't live in Manhattan any more (sigh). I can't entertain any more because of my living situation. But I still don't feel the urge to go berserk on holidays. I spend them quietly, usually alone and just smile indulgently as the advertisers try to convince me to spend my last nickel on overconsumption because "it's a holiday." I stay away from the lakes on the 4th of July here, and we have beautiful lakes in Tennessee, because of all the crazy drunks littering and racing boats. I will shoot off a few fireworks this evening I found while I was cleaning out the attic the other day. I hung out the flag on the huge maple tree out front, which I do whenever the holiday calls for a flag. And that's it. I'd love to make ice cream and have a barbecue for five or six friends, but I can't do that now. It's all right. It's not fatal. I will instead work on an important document I need to get done professionally.

For the millennium? I'll probably stay home and spend it the way I do all New Year's Eves these days. I'll listen to some music and go to bed early. I haven't been awake at midnight for New Year's in five or six years. (This is the original party person speaking.) I will not struggle over drinking and try to use the millennium as an excuse to make a fool of myself. I noticed an article recently where I believe the New York Philharmonic is giving a concert that evening up to midnight. If I were in New York, that's where I'd be that evening probably. And I would enjoy it. That's the sort of thing sane, civilized people do. It is not what drunks do. The whole world does not get drunk every holiday, despite what the liquor industry would have you believe.

Carl W.

I just had the first of many holiday celebrations on Sunday. Around 50 English teachers and their families. There was wine and beer there, and that was it.

I suppose people were drinking. I didn't really notice because I was too busy having fun. In fact, I was dancing (sometimes alone -- what the hell, there was a great band playing 50s music and I felt like dancing) and nearly fell off my chair laughing at all the stories about teaching experiences being told at my table.

It was actually more fun than I've had at a party in quite a few years, certainly better than the ones last year where I couldn't wait to get home and do some real drinking (a real closet case, I was).

Anyway, arrived at work this morning to discover that the head of the system has decreed that this year's party will be -- alcohol-FREE.

Maybe I can convince the teacher's organization that our next party can be alcohol free. People certainly didn't need it to have a good time, plus the money comes out of our annual dues!

C.A. E.

> *<I found that when cravings hit, posting a quick note saying I was having a hard time helped. Sitting in front of the computer, reading the responses would keep me busy and out of the store. There was always something in those responses that helped me stay strong, and remember why I was not drinking.>*

Am in 1OO% agreement with you on that, Jennifer. The same 'tool' is equally helpful for staying away from cigarettes when the going gets hard, for distancing oneself from any addiction I expect.

Seasonal tools for me include putting addresses on envelopes for soon-to-be-sent greeting cards and beginning to wrap Christmas gifts. May be doing at least the latter well in advance, but no harm to that and I'M NOT SMOKING.

Anne

I do this also, and am actually logged on this moment because I was getting the Xmas decorations out of the attic, had some up, and was getting the tree out and started to want a drink. Haven't had one of these spells in a while. So I am doing what I have done for over a year now, grab a soda and run to SOS. And to have these particular posts today, well, Santa Claus works in mysterious ways.

Shirl

The first time around for me, about 5 years into it, I called off the holidays due to lack of interest. I was tired of doing the card/gift exchange thing. And to help bolster my emotional sobriety, I quit doing it. Hardly anybody missed the cards, and those that did got a personal New Year's Greeting.

As for gifts, I started a tradition of putting together some packages for homeless folks and telling folks that I usually exchanged presents with to please do the same instead of buying me a gift.

What is nice about this husband is he understands that the holidays are just as miserable for me as they are supposed to be happy. I even seemed to enjoy them last year without the urging to be Holiday Cheerful.

De W.

I support and applaud your use of Christmas rituals and activities (writing cards, wrapping presents) as sobriety tools. Those sorts of activities, I imagine, can help folks to stay productively involved, focused, and abstinent. I support "whatever works" and I think you offer good examples and sound advice.

However, I think it is also important to ring in for the "other side" of the phenomenon where the holidays season is stressing, upsetting, disappointing, and depressing for untold numbers of nice people. More significantly and dangerous psychologically, it becomes "crazy making" as the gigantic propaganda machine ("It's a Wonderful Life" and the 1001 versions of "A Christmas Carol") pressure people to "get into the spirit," to operate with increased levity, to experience "good will toward men," and most crazy-making of all, to recapture the feelings associated with some idealized or fantasized memories of Christmases long past.

Don't get me wrong, I'm not knocking "good will toward men," but I don't think it is something that you can just "switch on" the day after you have stuffed yourself with Thanksgiving turkey because the Hallmark Greeting Card Company says that you should.

It may sound silly, but I think it is worth noting that Jimmy Stewart (love the man) was an actor playing a role in "It's a Wonderful Life!" I am certain that at the time, none of those people had any idea they were making a great American classic -- and when the film was completed, they all went back to being the strange creatures that actors are when they are not working! They probably shot the movie in June BTW.

The film was a great collaborative effort with the specific intention of creating an illusion that would evoke a particular set of emotional responses from the audience. It is called "art." In this case, they created exceptionally good art, probably without realizing it. But art and reality are often very far apart. And I guess all I am suggesting is to enjoy the experience of having your heart strings tugged at -- savor the archetype -- without losing sight of the fact that the director and the players are fucking with your head. The simplicity, charm and "redemption" of "It's a Wonderful Life" (et al.), are something most people are unlikely to ever experience in their life except at the movies.

If you "can't get it up" for the holidays, don't panic, and don't blame yourself. There are literally more than 2 billion (That is 2,000,000,000....two thousand million...10 times the population of the United States) Jews, Muslims, Buddhists, Hindus, militant atheists, and others who don't give a shit about this stuff, and who perceive the American "holiday season" as slightly mad. Historians may very well look back on the American Christmas season in the 20th Century as a manifestation of mass psychosis!

Contrary to what my post may suggest, I don't play the scrooge during the holidays. I have experimented with that, and it just makes me feel worse! But I do operate ruthlessly on the "KISS" (Keep it simple, stupid!) principle. Here's my list:

1. I keep it simple, stupid!
2. I maintain modest expectations.
3. I do a little, not a lot.
4. I try to do what pleases me, not others -- and look for a workable compromise when the two conflict.
5. I keep social visits short.
6. I keep to a minimum the stressors of crowds, traffic, jammed shopping malls, and travel. I use the internet a lot.
7. I don't spend much money on presents. To the extent that it is possible, I try to choose small, but meaningful gifts.
8. I like sending cards, but I don't send so many that it taxes my energy or my pocket book.
9. I don't pig-out on holiday meals and snack food. I try to exercise every day regardless of other demands of the season.
10. I don't drink or use drugs, not matter what.

Mahalo nui loa & aloha,

Happy Holidays!

Rex

The holidays have always been my worst time of year. This year, which will ideally be my first sober December, is already pressing its evil little insinuations of "Everyone else is so happy, it must just be you" and the like. I hate this more than anything else in the world.

I recently came off of a very difficult time, as many of you know, and then got sober again but isolated (hard). I finally feel ready to rejoin the world. Unfortunately, I decided to join just in time for ... THE HOLIDAYS.

I've not yet decided any real strategy for maintaining my sobriety, although I am shoplifting ideas from y'all liberally, and will continue to do so.

Chris "I will not be pushed, filed, stamped, indexed, briefed, debriefed or numbered."

Chris

I seem to recall Christmas being a difficult time for me from around age 18 to 24. It was during this time that I was with an idiot for a boyfriend, who wasn't welcome in my parents' home. It was only when I left him at age 24 that Christmas began to get better.

Unfortunately that was when I began drinking a lot, and although I know I always had a control problem with drinking, it was then that it started to become a more serious problem. I suppose mainly for the reason that through ages 18-24 I was just partying along with the rest of the crowd, doing what everyone else did, but at 24 I started to mature somewhat, and found myself with more responsibilities at work and at home. The increase in my drinking habit did not help.

So, for the past 5 years or so, the holidays have been a big drinking ordeal. Lots of fun and lots of booze. My family always has a lot of liquor around the house, and we all indulge around holiday time. It's just another excuse for me to drink. (Amazing how those excuses added up and melded into one 5 year or more long, continuous excuse).

Not to say that my family is a bunch of drunks, but they do enjoy their "holiday cheer." They would never address someone's (my) drinking problem unless it was directly physically affecting them or hurting them. They would prefer to laugh it off rather than "stick their nose in."

I was pretty good at keeping my alcoholism a secret, and they either didn't see it or chose not to. Likely the latter. When I finally admitted to them that I am an alkie and told them I was quitting, they were not surprised, and somewhat relieved, I think.

This will be my first sober Christmas as long as I can remember (or not, *laugh*).... I really don't know how it's going to go. As I read the posts regarding the holidays I feel distant and disconnected from the entire holiday issue. I think I'm ignoring it. I'd like to obtain some sort of holiday enthusiasm, but I'm afraid it will just lead me down a road of cravings and confusion that I don't care to follow.

On the other hand, I love Christmastime. I want to put up decorations, and go shopping, and see the children, and enjoy my first Xmas with my husband, as a married couple. It's supposed to be special. In a lot of ways it will be, including the fact that it will be my first sober one, and I know I should take all the negatives and turn them into positives.

I don't want to disappoint my husband, who is really looking forward to a Yuletide Christmas with all the fixings, as he never really got any of that in the past. His family was very poor, his parents divorced and both alcoholics. Since meeting me, he says he finally feels a sense of family again. I don't want to diminish that by boycotting Christmas, but part of me really wants to just keep ignoring it, till it passes. I did it with Halloween and it was so much easier....

Treena

I have the choice to use, or not. Everyday I wake, and I make a conscious decision to remain clean and sober. I am sure I am thinking about this choice in my sleep as well because my dreams are often filled with many bizarre using behaviors etc. This priority of my way of life leads into decisions about all other areas. I can "play" the games, i.e. holiday stuff, co-workers "good-bye" rituals, and on and on, or NOT "play."

Why all the fretting about this time of the year etc.? I learned to say NO. And as the saying doesn't go ... JUST DON'T DO IT!!!!!!!!!!!

In my experience x-job, x-co-workers, x-friends, x-family, x-using buddies, x-etc., do not really give a ___. Anyone that wants to come over and ride horses with me today (clean and sober and no smoking) come on!

Nancy

I've had good and bad Christmases sober, but definitely nowhere near as bad as when I was drinking. Thing is, we don't put up trees, decorations, or anything. We usually don't even buy each other presents except a token present like a couple of shares of stock or something.

Since my wife's birthday is Christmas Eve, I always get her a nice B-day present -- but that's about it. To me it's a weird religious holiday with rather odd pagan symbolism attached, and I see no reason to accept it uncritically. I figure if I'm going to put up with this weird holiday, I'll take what I want and leave the rest. I no longer have tolerance for myself getting down over this stupid cultural ritual, and if anybody on this SECULAR list has a problem with that then I say SCROOGE YOU. :)

If you continue to take it one day at a time, then Xmas is just one more day. Right? Why make it a whole month of days? Lucky Rex [in Thailand] probably doesn't even have to see those drunken Santas outside the malls ringing the bells.

Bah Humbug! :-)

Jim Y

Many of us who celebrate a secular, 'family-time' Christmas are actually being rather true to the original Winter Solstice tidings. The Yule Log, decoration of trees, mistletoe, family (clan) gatherings, etc. are all related to the old pagan celebration. Indiscriminate sex and lots of alcohol were also part of it, so you could say that even the office Christmas party 'harkens to an earlier time.' The partying would last days on end -- possibly weeks.

It's my understanding that Christmas was placed so close to the solstice intentionally by the early Christian high mucky-mucks, to cut down on the debauchery. If we have any religious scholars among us, please correct me if I'm mistaken about this.

So, a Happy Winter Solstice to all -- but leave out the booze. It'll leave you awake longer for the other debaucheries....

Marjorie

Here in Japan, Christmas Eve is celebrated by:

1) a bucket of Kentucky Fried Chicken (and the Colonel Sanders standing in front of the joints wear little Santa Claus outfits),

2) a frosted Christmas cake decorated with gaudy swirls and figurines,

3) champagne (a non-alcoholic version is available for

the kiddies).

Fried chicken and cake is now such a tradition that burger joints, convenience stores, almost every place imaginable has tables with piles of boxes readily packaged for carrying home on the subways and trains. (I always wondered what happened to all of the decorated cakes the day after because by Dec. 26th they've all miraculously disappeared.)

Oh, one other thing: the person you sleep with on Christmas Eve supposedly remains your sweetheart for a long time, so the love hotels are crowded with young couples.

Actually, as a singer, I was always pretty busy around Christmastime. Last year, for the first time, our chorus participated in a Christmas concert with a well-known conductor from Tokyo. We did some of the usual Christmas stuff -- Silent Night, the Hallelujah chorus, and the piece about 14 angels from Humperdinck's Hansel and Gretel. The program also included Battle Hymn of the Republic as the climax before the intermission, and it got a huge round of applause.

This year we'll just be doing the traditional December classical piece, Beethoven's 9th.

And that's Christmas in Japan. Ho, ho, ho!

-- C.A. E.

Hello, all. I have my first sober holiday woe, and I was wondering if you all might have some insight into how to handle it.

My wife is a huge fan of the holidays and was planning on having a Christmas party at our place as an alternative to her annual work party. Since I passed out at last year's alternative work party, I became keenly aware of two things: (1) the party was going to include alcohol and (2) it was going to be at our house.

End result: the party is on ice (for now), but I can't help feeling that I am to blame. Questions such as "am I being oversensitive" and "am I blowing this out of proportion" keep nagging at me. While my wife is willing to not have the party in order to accommodate my wishes, and is being very understanding by not pressing the issue, I feel like an ass.

Any thoughts?

Brad

You are not an ass -- at least as far as not wanting the party -- I don't know about other areas ;-). But seriously, your sobriety IS very important (I assume it is, because you care enough about it to ask this question), and it's clear from your concerns that having such a party at your home could easily be threatening to your sobriety.

If you had emphysema, would you feel like an ass if a smoker in your home no longer smoked in the home because of your breathing problems? Maybe 30 years ago, when the social acceptance of smoking still outweighed the health concerns that were recently emerging, some people would have been offended had you asked them not to smoke around you. Perhaps it's still that way with drinking, but then, those who would be offended are likely the ones with a drinking problem themselves. I certainly don't think you should feel bad about it, and you should have every right to keep an atmosphere you find harmful (whether literal or figurative) out of your own home.

It may be a good idea to talk this over with your wife, and express your feelings with her, and also thank her for not putting pressure on you about having the party. You might want to consider having/announcing a no-alcohol-allowed party — you may not feel totally comfortable being at a party without drinking, but you may meet some people whom you become friends with, that you would never meet any other way.

Ben B.

And well you should feel uncomfortable. In fact, panic would be understandable.

A few years back we had a solstice party at our house. We made it clear on the invitations (in small but distinct print) that this would be a no-alcohol affair. It was an amazing educational experience for me. I learned three things.

1. People will come to parties even if there is no alcohol there. Amazing as it may seem, people have other motives for coming to parties besides getting drunk, such as the pleasure of seeing us and each other, companionship, having a good time, catching up on gossip, flirting, relaxing with friends -- stuff like that.
2. A party will go into a roar even without alcohol there. People start talking and that starts more people talking and then people talk louder to be heard over the other people talking and pretty soon the place is reverberating with that familiar party roar that warms the heart of the host and hostess.
3. I was able to have a good time and be witty and outrageous and friendly and outgoing and all those things I never am in reality, without a drop of alcohol in my system. I just sort of got a 'contact high' from all those sober people having a great time.

We alcoholics tend to have a highly perverted sense of fun. This is, in a biochemical sense, our root problem. See the Kenneth Blum article, Reward Deficiency Syndrome, on www.unhooked.com. Our codependents, even without being hooked on the chemical, tend to share our worldview. This blind spot in our view of pleasure blocks us from seeing that "alcohol" and "fun" are not equivalents. We should know by now very well that we can have (a) without (b). But it takes us longer to learn that we can very well also have (b) without (a).

If I had a vote, I'd say have the party but make it alcohol and drug free. BTW that has the added advantage that you can invite kids to the party, which makes it easier on parents to come. The sheer novelty of the concept will bring people out. And quite a few people will quietly thank you afterward. Holiday office parties are a nightmare for lots of people, especially the women in the office, who have to fend off the horny drunk males. Your boss may even give you a bonus (unless the boss is a drunk, of course).

Marty

Be very, very grateful that your wife is willing to accommodate you on this one, quit feeling like an ass, and forget about the party without another thought. Maybe after you have several sober years under your belt, you might want to revisit this issue, but I doubt it even then.

After 20+ years of being sober, I finally feel comfortable enough to serve the occasional drink in my house now, but I wouldn't for a moment consider hosting a holiday bash where heavy drinking would be almost inevitable. Hell, I wouldn't ever consider going to somebody else's bash, unless I knew for sure that I could safely escape early, long before the drinking kicks into high gear.

Make it up to your wife somehow, in some way that doesn't involve alcohol, but please, don't flirt with this sort of disaster. And don't feel like an ass -- it doesn't have to be a BFD if you don't let it; your friends will not miss one more Christmas party, and you will not become social pariahs because of it.

Sorry for coming on so strong -- usually I at least try to make my free advice sound like something else -- but this is dynamite you're playing with, and you'd be very lucky if all you lost were your fingers. Christmas was always the time when my drinking ran wild -- it isn't just a coincidence that my birthday comes just before Christmas -- and I am still always extra-careful around the holiday season. Burn those invitations, quick!

Larry

This is a tough one, that hits close to home. It was really hard for my partner to accept that I am addicted to alcohol. If I would just not drink so much, there wouldn't be a problem, right? In the beginning, she didn't really seem all that pleased with my sobriety. She would invite me to drinking events and be somewhat disappointed when I didn't want to go. It's as if she had forgotten all the broken promises I had made while drinking, (not only about drinking but other things I would promise to change), the embarrassing situations, the missed work, the missed deadlines, the no money, etc. See Keepers list of 365 reasons.

This was hard to do, but I slowly and gently (without beating myself up) reminded her of some of those bad times, and how some of us get addicted to the stuff and have a really hard time giving it up. Would you invite a heroin or cocaine addict to a party where using was one of the main activities? Because of alcohol being legal and part of our culture, we don't think of it that way, unless you're addicted like us.

It took months before she realized how much better a partner I am without alcohol. It has resulted in changes in our social schedule, but the more positive experiences we have without drinking (me not drinking in particular), the easier it is for her to accept the things I don't feel comfortable with.

Even with months of sobriety under my belt, the thought of a party in the house makes me very uncomfortable. Your apprehension is a warning signal that should not be ignored.

Over the holidays you may end up in other unavoidable situations where alcohol is served. These are a few of my tools:

A couple of "nuts and bolts" things that really help me out when I do end up at an event where alcohol is served:

1. Keep a non-alcohol drink in your hand at all times.
2. Be prepared with what you are going to do when someone opens a beer or mixes a drink, and sticks it in your hand. It has happened to me. Be prepared to get very firm.
3. Reflect back on the people you know that don't drink much or any, and seek out their company. This has been very enriching to me, as I think many of them have wanted to talk to me in the past, but I was too blotto.
4. If you're starting to feel a little thirsty, like maybe one drink might take the edge off the nervousness, signal your partner to leave. Work out a code word beforehand. This is why I personally support your decision not to have the party at your house. If you're in trouble, you got nowhere to go.
5. Be prepared for the questions about why you are not drinking. This has been a point of debate lately on the SOS email group. Personally, I just say doctor's orders, and leave it at that. I discuss my alco-

> holism with my closest friends only, and don't feel comfortable discussing it with acquaintances at parties.

Its not easy Brad, but the most important thing is to stay sober, no matter what. And staying sober may mean no parties at the house for now.

I apologize in advance if this seems judgmental in any way, it's just that it hit a chord with me and my situation.

Don

I am seeing lots of good "stuff" coming from all quarters in answer to your post. I, too, was always nuts about the holidays; went crazy with the decorations, etc. etc. I especially like Don's planning ahead, since having "a plan" has been a critical part in my staying sober.

Something you and your wife might consider as a compromise would be an alternative, such as

1. Having a small group over, and going Christmas caroling.
2. Having a small group over for a formal, sit down dinner (catered, of course!)

This may sound sort of goofy, but the supermarkets are now awash in magazines giving ideas about holiday entertaining. Woman's Day, Family Circle, and others, have plenty ideas for entertaining that have "no-alcohol" alternatives. Just think, as well, that the sight of a man buying such mags will set hearts a-flutter throughout the store! Just joking, of course.

I hope that this helps; if nothing more than knowing that you have a lot of company in the "squirmy season" as I call it. Fond regards,

Bones

My own take is not to do this party if possible. It's way too early, or would be for me, especially, as you point out, that there's no viable escape route. If you're gonna have a party, I like the idea of trying it alcohol-free.

As for the idea that you're being an ass and blowing this out of proportion: Absolutely NOT. This is not just worrying about what some people you only sort of know will think of you. It's about your life and how YOU will think of you.

I think it's great that you're keeping your sobriety at the front end of this thing. I am also facing my first sober holiday season in a while and am none too comfortable about it. All I really know is that I will not drink.

Bill M.

As another newbie with just 9 weeks sober, I am beginning to understand how difficult it is to stay sober, especially at this time of year. I still have a lot of folks around me who don't want to accept the fact that I don't drink any more (it's soooo out of character for me, after all!).

My worst times are the evenings when I'm alone because my partner is out of town on business. I wish there were a meeting in my area, because I would give anything for an hour just to talk. When I tried to get into the chat area, after all the stuff you have to go through to get on to it, I was given the message that my poor computer is just too out of date to play there. (You'll have to excuse me, I'm not real computer literate yet). So, so far I've been mostly lurking on this list. It helps, but I wish I could figure out a way to start a group so that I have somewhere to physically go to talk. Anyone have some feedback??

Sue

I made it through last year very self-consciously and felt like a displaced person. I'm more comfortable this year with my sobriety, I can even order an NA drink without stumbling over saying it. Like a lot of us I just live an average suburban lifestyle and I don't have a Ph.D. in English language. I don't hang out in dark and dingy bars.

I do have friends who will invite us over for a dinner party and yes, when everyone is enjoying their glass of wine I envy them at times. Yes, when I go to this wedding tomorrow and 249 people are toasting with champagne in their glasses, a part of me will want to have some too.

I don't envy the getting drunk and feeling like shit the

next day, which I know will happen to most of them and me too if I started. Yes on Thanksgiving I will want my customary brandy Alexander, but I'm getting better at it. So it's all those little occasions that come up that are dangerous and I have to be on guard.

If that is called obsessing over it well, gee I am an alcoholic after all and thinking about having a drink does pop into my mind now and then.

Shirl

The best option is sometimes just staying home. However, I know that realistically, this isn't always going to happen, so....

BYOB -- I bring seltzer and a lemon and lime to all family occasions. I make a big glass as soon as I get there and always keep it full so no one has the chance to ask me "Can I get you a drink?"

I avoid getting in discussions that I know are volatile or will upset me. If there is a situation that is stressing me, I just leave the room. I also take a walk around the block alone with my husband and kids after the meal. It's a nice relaxing way to recharge my batteries.

Make a list of the reasons you don't want to/can't drink anymore, and keep it in your pocket. Look at if you need reminding.

Remember you have the best reason of all to be thankful -- You are sober!

Jennifer

I think I'm going to keep Xmas low-key this year. In the past it has been a big drinking family thing. This is not to say I'm not going to attend the Xmas eve party at my sis' place or the Xmas dinner at mom and dad's ... I'm just going to try to keep myself in a mellow state the entire time, keep reminding myself and enjoying what is good without alcohol.

I find club soda and lemon to work well too. It has a bitter taste, so it's sippable like wine. White grape juice mixed with club soda is a good champagne substitute. You can even add a bit of orange juice to have with breakfast. :-)

Treena

Good ideas Treen! New Year's Eve is also our wedding anniversary. It's always been a big party night -- alcohol, drugs, sex. I won't be doing any of those this year! I always had champagne & orange juice for breakfast New Year's Day. I'll try your substitute this year. I'd love any other suggestions for ways to celebrate. I'd like to start some new traditions this year, alcohol & drug free ones. Any ideas??

Jennifer

I am not sure what it is, but there is this emotional quagmire associated with the American Christmas holidays that I just hate. And even if I can manage to tippy-toe around the quagmire, I cannot entirely avoid the impact from other people who are having emotional problems with it.

Maybe it is the underlying Christian resurrection myth. After all, "A Christmas Carol" as well as "It's a Wonderful Life" are both stories of resurrection where the meanies and the despondent are swiftly and magically transformed into warm-blooded creatures, filled with gratitude and a new zest for living! Although I can appreciate "It's a Wonderful Life" as a fine and classic example of American film making (I love film), I wonder how many broke, lonely old guys have blown their brains out as they sat watching that stupid movie for the umpteenth Christmas, upset that they don't feel all "warm & fuzzy."

Anyway, my Christmas Carol, sung to the tune of "Joy to the World" is

"Lower your expectations, and you'll feel better!"

Write the rest yourself!

Rex

The next two months are the grand time for depression and alcohol. I've made it through the last two years without succumbing to either and even found that holiday parties were much more satisfying as places to enjoy others sober than when I was flying through the throng in my Sopwith Camel (?).

The whole jostling-jingly superficiality of it all used to lead me to the scotch as fast as possible. It would seem that if we all put up enough decorations (sorry Martha Stewart), there will be real festivity and good feelings. The next day comments seem to me to say much: "What a lovely tree (do you know the origin of those shiny balls that are on the tannenbaum?) and, oh my, the food was delicious." Not a lot about the possibility of the joy of being human.

I recall in college being told by a fraternity brother: "You gotta believe." "No, I don't," I replied. Seems to have stayed with me. This can create isolation, so I have learned to be a somewhat Boston politician who can banter and roll with it. Now that I don't drink, much of the absurdity and humor if it all is very pleasant. But sometimes I feel that I am living through a period of Christmas letters that merely want to tell me that the writer has gone to France and the wines were so good.

I sometimes think that here in Amerika we live from one holiday to another, as though life were centered on preparation for them and then on to the next. This is like constantly living an anticipatory life with nothing alive, yet.

MOG

My most unusual Christmas sober was about 4 years ago.

The employer I was working for at the time had decided to have the Christmas party at a nice restaurant near the airport. My wife and I finally found the place as the road it's on isn't well lighted.

We got there midway through the cocktail hour, as I'd planned. So Far, So Good.

I got a soft drink for my wife and I. Sat with a friend and her husband who I knew were only social drinkers. Talked a while, then ordered dinner. Had another soft drink or two.

Watched the evening progress as people imbibing got

stupider and stupider as the booze hit their systems.

After dinner was finished, we hung around for a while. I had about 3 cups of coffee with dinner and afterwards.

We left around 10:30, as our son wasn't well and we wanted to get home to him. Made our way out to the car. We laughed over the fact that my boss and one of the senior managers had on the same tacky, loud, LED-lighted tie.

As we sat in the car, just before leaving to go home, I asked my wife how much I'd drank in the evening. She tallied up 3 ginger ale and 3 coffee. I said to her to imagine adding 1 to 2 ounces of rye to each glass of ginger ale, and about an ounce of brandy to each coffee. Her eyes widened.

I chuckled. "Dear, if I had consumed that much, in that short a period, you'd be sitting in the car with me passed out in the driver's seat wondering how the hell we were going to get home because you don't drive!"

We then laughed and headed for home ... cold, stone sober.

Don G

Order Form

Please send _____ copy(ies) of **Keepers** to:

Name: ____

Addr. 1: ____

Addr. 2: ____

City, State, Zip: ____________________________________

Price per copy:	**$12.00**
Californians, add sales tax per copy:	**$0.99**
Priority Mail Shipping per copy:	**$3.20**

Total enclosed: **$**__________________

Order directly from

LifeRing Press
1440 Broadway Suite 1000
Oakland, CA 94612-2029
Tel: 510-763-0779
Fax: 510-763-1513
Email: publisher@lifering.com

Or Order Online: www.lifering.com

Ask About Meeting Discounts